William Henry Furness

The story of the Resurrection of Christ

William Henry Furness

The story of the Resurrection of Christ

ISBN/EAN: 9783742811301

Manufactured in Europe, USA, Canada, Australia, Japa

Cover: Foto ©Lupo / pixelio.de

Manufactured and distributed by brebook publishing software (www.brebook.com)

William Henry Furness

The story of the Resurrection of Christ

THE STORY

OF THE

RESURRECTION OF CHRIST

TOLD ONCE MORE

WITH

REMARKS UPON THE CHARACTER OF CHRIST
AND THE HISTORICAL CLAIMS OF THE FOUR GOSPELS

BY

WILLIAM H. FURNESS D.D.

PHILADELPHIA
J. B. LIPPINCOTT & CO.
1885

Copyright, 1884, by J. B. LIPPINCOTT & Co.

TO

MY BROTHERS

IN

THE MINISTRY OF THE CHRISTIAN FAITH

THESE PAGES

ARE

RESPECTFULLY INSCRIBED.

THE STORY OF THE RESURRECTION

THE STORY OF THE RESURRECTION.

It is now more than fifty years ago that, in reading the accounts of the most extraordinary Event in the history of Christ, the Event upon which the Apostles laid the greatest stress, the corner-stone of primitive Christianity: the Reappearance of Christ alive after death, it came to me that what the guard at the Sepulchre mistook for a figure alighting from heaven, and the women believed to be an angel, was no other than Jesus himself.

What suggested this thought was a particular in the Story, slight indeed, but it struck me as very significant: the special mention of Peter in the message sent to the disciples by the supposed angel, "Go tell his disciples *and Peter* that Jesus is risen." I seemed to hear the voice of Jesus in this singling out of that disciple, whose last act had been to swear that he did not know him. Although thus shamefully disowned by his cowardly friend, Jesus made haste to assure him that the past was not remembered against him, that he was not disowned in return as he might well fear that he would be. To the fact that Jesus had risen, no angel could testify so impressively, it seemed to me, as this message to Peter, in such keeping is it with the greatness of mind that characterized Jesus.

Once possessed with the idea that it was not an angel but Jesus himself whom the guard and the women saw, I seemed to have found the key which opened the whole Story to the light, the light of Truth and Nature illumining it to its minutest details, all unconsciously, on the part of the narrators. As I read it now, overflowing as it is with evidence of its truth which no one thought of furnishing, it seems to have written itself.

The more I have pondered it, the more deeply have I been impressed by its wonderful internal evidence. If the actual Re-appearance of Jesus alive in the flesh to Mary is not proved, then nothing in the Gospels is proved, nothing in all the world. All is an illusion.

From time to time, in various publications, I have told the Story as I read it. I am going to tell it once more, not only because there are certain new lights to throw upon it, but mainly because I cannot resist its inexhaustible attraction. Is it only a fancy that I am gratifying? or is it a conviction of truth?

There are certain preliminary considerations to be attended to.

1. I assume the entire honesty of the narrators. That they may have been mistaken as to what was seen and heard, I readily concede. But that they meant to deceive, or to tell what they did not believe to be true, I find no shadow of a reason for suspecting.

2. It is equally certain that between the four different accounts of the first Appearance of Jesus there is no collusion. Their glaring discrepancies show on the very face of them that they are four independent reports.

3. Although I consider it very remarkable

that Jesus is never described as appearing in the glory with which I cannot but think he would have been represented as arrayed, were his re-appearances the creations of the imagination inspired by the love of the marvellous, I am free to say that I do not find in the accounts of the subsequent appearances of the risen Christ, the same striking evidence of truth that I find in the accounts of his first appearance. This first appearance, however, being established, a presumption is created in favor of the truth of the after-appearances.

4. Believing in the actual Resurrection of Christ, I freely admit that questions may be asked which I cannot answer. But what one thing is there in nature, which, even when set forth in the full blaze of the most advanced Science, does not suggest questions for which we have no solution? Have we got so far in understanding everything that we have a right to make it the condition of our acceptance of any extraordinary fact, however well attested, that it shall leave nothing unexplained? Where was Jesus after death when he did not appear to his disciples? What was the mode of his existence then? I

cannot even conjecture. What finally became of him? The common belief is that he ascended visibly into the sky. But there is not in the four Gospels a word that necessitates this idea. Neither in the first Gospel, nor in the fourth, and these happen to be the only ones ascribed to personal disciples of Christ, is anything said of a final disappearance. The second Gospel, in the closing verses, which, by the way, are of questionable genuineness, states briefly that Jesus was received up into heaven, and sate at the right hand of God. Such was evidently the belief. We are not required to understand this brief statement as meaning to say that he was seen taken up into the sky and seated at the right hand of God. The third Gospel says that he "led his disciples out as far as Bethany, and he lifted up his hands and blest them, and while he blest them, he was parted from them, and carried up into heaven." In the book of the Acts we read that "a cloud hid him from sight, and he was taken up into heaven." Neither of these accounts necessarily signifies that he ascended visibly. When he disappeared the natural conclusion was that he had gone to heaven.

The language of these histories on this point is significant. It tells us what was believed. But there is not a word going to show that they undertake to localize the place of the departed. They state only a popular belief.

5. Whatever difficulties are involved in any event, however extraordinary it may be, we are bound to accept it, when it rests upon irrefragable evidence. Such is the case with the Resurrection of Christ. I cannot tell what his condition was after he rose from the dead, or where he was when not seen, or whither he went. It is an article of the popular creed, by the way, that he descended into hell. It has no foundation in the Gospels. If I were under the necessity of believing either that he ascended or descended, I should rather incline to think that he went down to save the lost; it would be much more like him than to go up into heaven to be seated on a throne with a crown of gold upon his head. The crown of thorns becomes him better. But be that as it may, that he re-appeared alive after death, and was seen and spoken with, the evidence has put it out of my power to doubt. To borrow words ascribed to

an eminent scientist in relation to some new phenomenon, "I do not say it is possible, I say it is true."

And now, as I relate what took place, on the early morning of the third day after the crucifixion of Jesus, in the garden where his body has been buried, it will be seen with what inimitable signatures of truth the original narratives are written all over, not by mortal hand, but by truth and nature.

I introduce here the passages in the Gospels from which the Story is gathered:

Matthew xxviii, 1–10.

In the end of the sabbath, as it began to dawn toward the first day of the week, came Mary Magdalene and the other Mary to see the sepulchre.

And, behold, there was a great earthquake: for the angel of the Lord descended from heaven, and came and rolled back the stone from the door, and sat upon it.

His countenance was like lightning, and his raiment white as snow:

And for fear of him the keepers did shake, and became as dead men.

And the angel answered and said unto the women, Fear not ye; for I know that ye seek Jesus, who was crucified.

He is not here: for he is risen, as he said. Come, see the place where the Lord lay.

And go quickly, and tell his disciples that he is risen from the dead; and, behold, he goeth before you into Galilee; there shall ye see him: lo, I have told you.

And they departed quickly from the sepulchre with fear and great joy; and did run to bring his disciples word.

And as they went to tell his disciples, behold, Jesus met them, saying, All hail. And they came and held him by the feet, and worshipped him.

Mark xvi, 1-10.

And when the sabbath was past, Mary Magdalene, and Mary the mother of James, and Sa-

THE STORY OF THE RESURRECTION.

lome, had bought sweet spices, that they might come and anoint him.

And very early in the morning the first day of the week, they came unto the sepulchre at the rising of the sun.

And they said among themselves, Who shall roll us away the stone from the door of the sepulchre?

And when they looked, they saw that the stone was rolled away: for it was very great.

And entering into the sepulchre, they saw a young man sitting on the right side, clothed in a long white garment; and they were affrighted.

And he saith unto them, Be not affrighted: Ye seek Jesus of Nazareth, who was crucified: he is risen; he is not here: behold the place where they laid him.

But go your way, tell his disciples and Peter that he goeth before you into Galilee: there shall ye see him, as he said unto you.

And they went out quickly, and fled from the sepulchre; for they trembled and were amazed:

neither said they any thing to any man; for they were afraid.

Now when Jesus was risen early the first day of the week, he appeared first to Mary Magdalene, out of whom he had cast seven devils.

And she went and told them that had been with him, as they mourned and wept.

Luke xxiv, 1–12.

Now upon the first day of the week, very early in the morning, they came unto the sepulchre, bringing the spices which they had prepared, and certain others with them.

And they found the stone rolled away from the sepulchre.

And they entered in, and found not the body of the Lord Jesus.

And it came to pass, as they were much perplexed thereabout, behold, two men stood by them in shining garments:

And as they were afraid, and bowed down their faces to the earth, they said unto them, Why seek ye the living among the dead?

He is not here, but is risen: remember how he spake unto you when he was yet in Galilee,

Saying, The Son of man must be delivered into the hands of sinful men, and be crucified, and the third day rise again.

And they remembered his words,

And returned from the sepulchre, and told all these things unto the eleven, and to all the rest.

It was Mary Magdalene, and Joanna, and Mary the mother of James, and other women that were with them, who told these things unto the apostles.

And their words seemed to them as idle tales, and they believed them not.

Then arose Peter, and ran unto the sepulchre; and stooping down, he beheld the linen clothes laid by themselves, and departed, wondering in himself at that which was come to pass.

John xx, 1-18.

The first day of the week cometh Mary Magdalene early, when it was yet dark, unto the sepulchre, and seeth the stone taken away from the sepulchre.

Then she runneth, and cometh to Simon Peter, and to the other disciple, whom Jesus loved, and saith unto them, They have taken away the Lord out of the sepulchre, and we know not where they have laid him.

Peter therefore went forth, and that other disciple, and came to the sepulchre.

So they ran both together: and the other disciple did outrun Peter, and came first to the sepulchre.

And he stooping down, and looking in, saw the linen clothes lying; yet went he not in.

Then cometh Simon Peter following him, and went into the sepulchre, and seeth the linen clothes lie,

And the napkin, that was about his head, not lying with the linen clothes, but wrapped together in a place by itself.

Then went in also that other disciple, which came first to the sepulchre, and he saw, and believed.

For as yet they knew not the scripture, that he must rise again from the dead.

Then the disciples went away again unto their own home.

But Mary stood without at the sepulchre weeping: and as she wept, she stooped down, and looked into the sepulchre,

And seeth two angels in white sitting, the one at the head, and the other at the feet, where the body of Jesus had lain.

And they say unto her, Woman, why weepest thou? She saith unto them, Because they have taken away my Lord, and I know not where they have laid him.

And when she had thus said, she turned herself back, and saw Jesus standing, and knew not that it was Jesus.

Jesus saith unto her, Woman, why weepest thou? whom seekest thou? She, supposing him to be the gardener, saith unto him, Sir, if thou have borne him hence, tell me where thou hast laid him, and I will take him away.

Jesus saith unto her, Mary. She turned herself, and saith unto him, Rabboni; which is to say, Master.

Jesus saith unto her, Touch me not; for I am not yet ascended to my Father: but go to my brethren, and say unto them, I ascend unto my Father, and your Father; and to my God, and your God.

Mary Magdalene came and told the disciples that she had seen the Lord, and that he had spoken these things unto her.

It was on the sixth day of the week, the day before the Jewish Sabbath, that the crucifixion of Jesus took place. Towards the close of the day, certain friends of his, not of the number of his personal disciples, with the permission of the Roman governor, took down the body from the Cross, and, wrapping it, according to Jewish custom, in a white shroud of linen, laid it in a new tomb, in which no one had been laid before, in a neighboring garden.

The sun of that darkened day of blood set and the night passed, and the sun rose again, and the

Sabbath stillness of the seventh day rested over the sepulchre, and the garden, and the city.

The disciples of the Crucified, plunged in despair, mourned, and wept. Overwhelmed by the one inexorable fact that he was dead, for whom they had forsaken their homes, and from whom they had fondly expected to receive a hundredfold in return, they were lost in thick darkness. What heart had they to turn for light to the future, or to the past? He whom they had looked up to as about to appear in all the magnificence of the Messiah and to make them judges in Israel, had suddenly vanished, covered with public shame,—dead, buried. What cared they,—it could only aggravate the anguish of their ruined hopes,—to recall anything he had specially said or promised? The great Promise, upon which they had been depending so implicitly, lay crushed in the sepulchre. All was over. There was nothing left for them but to go heart-broken home to Galilee. Only some women, who had come with Jesus to the great city, agreed to go early the next morning to his tomb and pay a last poor tribute of affection to the dead.

While the disciples were thus stunned, stupefied by grief, the Priests, having compassed the destruction of Jesus, as they believed, under every circumstance of shame and horror, exulted in their triumph. Now they breathed freely. The man who had been such a terror to them, whose bold speech had lashed them into a frenzy of fear and hatred, was no more. They trusted that they had heard the last of him. To make all sure, however, and that there might be no possibility of any further imposture, they obtained from Pilate a guard to keep watch at the tomb. Certain things said by Jesus, as we may suppose, had come to their ears, through Judas possibly,—he had sold himself to them;—or, as Jesus had been rumored to have called the dead to life, and as they regarded him as one of the pretended Messiahs likely to appear at that time of excited popular expectation, they naturally conceived the suspicion that his adherents might plot some further imposition,—steal the body, and then give out that he had come to life. So they took the precaution of having the sepulchre watched.

Thus the Sabbath passed undisturbed by the

tumultuous crowds that had gathered around the man from Galilee wherever and whenever he appeared in public.

But, as the morning of the first day of the week was breaking, what strange story was that which came startling the Chief Priests? Into the city and to the house of the High Priest rushed the guard who had been stationed at the tomb, with wild, affrighted looks, in breathless accents declaring that there had been a great earthquake, and that the stone that closed the tomb had been rolled away by a figure that came down from heaven with eyes like lightning and raiment white as snow.

I pause here for a moment over this report of the guard. Strauss rejects the whole story of a watch set over the sepulchre as a fabrication designed to help prove the Resurrection of Jesus.

That there may be mistakes, great mistakes, indeed, and exaggerations in the Gospels, I concede. It would be strange if there were not, since events so exciting as those are which they record could hardly fail to excite the imagination and interfere with the power of accurate observation. Indeed, mistakes and exaggerations are not only to be looked for, they are important witnesses to the substantial truth of the narrative. When extraordinary events occur, they are always accompanied by false rumors and exaggerated statements. But the obviously artless character of the Gospels forbids us to charge them with such deliberate fabrications as Strauss and Renan do not hesitate to attribute to them.

Was the story told by the watch invented in order to help prove the Resurrection of Jesus? It makes no mention of him. It does not say that any one was seen to come from the tomb. Thus at the very point at which it should fulfil the purpose for which it is alleged that it was invented, it falls silent and entirely fails. If invented to support the Resurrection of Jesus, it should have made the guard report that some one entered the sepulchre or came out of it. As it is, if invented with a fraudulent design, it would really seem to have been fabricated in the interest of the Priests rather than of the disciples of Jesus. It certainly gave plausibility to the explanation which the Priests found of the affair, an explanation so plausible that it long gained currency among the Jews.

The report of the guard evidently struck the Priests as monstrous and incredible. Had it been ever so convincing of the fact that Jesus had returned to life, they would not have credited it. They had gone too far; they were committed to the denial of its truth. As it was, the men who told this strange story were plainly under the exaggerating influence of mortal terror. Their looks, their accents, and the story itself bore every mark of extreme fright. Had there been "a great earthquake," it would surely have been felt in the city. The natural and strong suspicion was that a trick had been played upon these men. Holding Jesus to be an impostor, having no faith in him, or in his adherents, the Priests soon found a solution of the matter: There had been a plot to steal the body, and the watch had been scared away that it might be carried off, and it could be given out that Jesus had come to life again. The guard, the Priests had no doubt, had fallen asleep. They may have done so, but it does not seem to me likely. Ignorant and superstitious, as they, doubtless, were, they were discharging the unaccustomed office of watching by night, at a grave, and at the grave of a man rumored to have possessed mysterious powers; there was everything to keep them awake. To the Priests it seemed certain that the men must have slumbered, and that a trick had been played upon them to scare them away from the spot.

Such was the Priests' solution of what had occurred. And this, substantially, was the story which they bribed the guard to tell, promising them immunity from punishment for sleeping on their watch, a promise which the Priests were confident they could fulfil, as they would make no complaint of the men to Pilate, and it was not a military duty the men had been set to discharge, nor had their alleged negligence had any result of any consequence in the eyes of the Roman authorities. Of course they were not required to say that they had been frightened away from the sepulchre. Strauss says it is incredible that the Sanhedrim should all agree to induce the guard to tell a falsehood. And it certainly is incredible. But it was not what the Priests regarded as a falsehood, but what, from their point of view, they honestly believed to be the truth, that they are reported to have urged the men to tell.

The question now comes: What was it that actually happened at the sepulchre? Something must have occurred to terrify the guard and cause them to flee from the spot with such an extraordinary story.

One circumstance, which the guard reported, we may credit without hesitation, namely, that the stone was removed from the sepulchre. So it was found by the women who came to the spot shortly afterwards.

As for the rest, the report of the guard betrays the magnifying influence of extreme terror. When men are frightened out of their senses, imagination rules the hour, and the simplest incidents are exaggerated into preternatural phenomena. Had there been a *great* earthquake, the women, who were on their way to the place, would have felt it, and so would the Priests in the neighboring city. But neither of these appear to have been aware of it.

It is worthy of note that the first particular that is mentioned is the earthquake. This it was that threw the guard into a paroxysm of affright. At that dark, still, lonely hour, as the guard naturally would be standing, sitting, or reclining, with their backs to the tomb, watching the approaches to the spot, they as naturally would be greatly startled by even a slight, sudden agitation of the ground. It could seem to them nothing less than the shock of an earthquake. I cannot avoid the conclusion that this jarring of the ground was caused by the removal of the stone.* The stone, used as a rude door to the sepulchre, was, I imagine, more or less of a slab-like description. As it fell away from its place, it caused a more or less violent concussion of the ground. If the stone were removed by some one standing outside of the tomb, he would have been seen by the guard, before the stone fell down. I believe, therefore, it was pushed away *from within* the sepulchre, which, obviously, could be done far more easily than it could be moved from without. The guard, startled by the jar thus caused, turned instinctively to the sepul-

---

* Dr. K. von Fritsch, of Halle, expresses the opinion that the causes of earthquakes are often much slighter than is commonly supposed, and supports it by facts. He states that quite feeble forces may produce agitations of the ground that will be felt at considerable distances.—*Popular Science Monthly*, No. 1, vol. xxi, p. 144.

chre. And there! a figure all in white appeared! The apparition, caught sight of as suddenly as the agitation of the earth was felt, completed their fright, and was nothing less, to eyes dilated by mortal terror, than a preternatural figure suddenly descended from heaven. What else could it be but Jesus himself in his long, white shroud?

As it was Jesus who removed the stone, we see why the earthquake is first mentioned. The jarring of the earth was felt before the figure appeared. Had the stone been moved by any one outside of the sepulchre, he would have been seen before the earthquake was felt, and then, it may be a question whether the guard would have felt the jarring of the ground caused by the stone, and then too there would have been no mention of an earthquake. As it was, it was the fright, caused by the agitation of the ground, that invested the figure that appeared with unearthly attributes.

The guard reported that the figure from heaven, having removed the stone, "*sat upon it.*" If, instead of an angel, it was Jesus who removed the stone, to seat himself was a natural position after the confinement in the sepulchre and the exertion of pushing away the stone.

The marvels that attended his previous career are marked by a severe simplicity strikingly in contrast with the exaggerations of fictions born of the imagination. There was nothing done by him merely to gratify the love of the wonderful. There never was any more power put forth than was absolutely necessary. When he recalled to life the young daughter of Jairus, she was not at once restored to perfect strength, as would have been represented were the story the creation of the imagination, which, once under the influence of the passion for the wonderful, scorns all limitations. Jesus directed that food should immediately be given her. Lazarus also needed instant assistance. Once, when the case of a blind man appealed to his compassion, as the man's infirmity prevented his being influenced by the commanding eye and air of Jesus, the restoration of his sight was, at the first word of Jesus, only partial. He was able to distinguish men, only by their walking, from trees. Then, as is related, Jesus spat on the ground and made clay with his saliva and applied it to the eyes of the blind man, not because there was any medicinal virtue in the application, but because it established a communication between the will of Jesus and the faith of the man which it stimulated into sanative action. Again, the demoniac of Gadara did not at once become sane at the bidding of Jesus. He became calm, but he still had the insane idea that a troop of foul spirits had possession of him, and he wanted ocular proof that they had left him; hence his insane request that the spirits should be sent into the swine. We read that at Nazareth, where he was brought up, Jesus did not many mighty works, "because of their unbelief." Had not faith been an essential factor in the marvels that he wrought, the unbelief of the Nazarenes was a reason why he should, not why he should not, have done mighty works there. But, faith being indispensable, he could work no wonders in a community that looked with contempt, born of familiarity, upon the son of the carpenter Joseph. They could not believe that he was, or could do, anything extraordinary.

That Jesus, then, should rest after the exertion of pushing away the stone from the sepulchre is a supposition not so fanciful as it may at first sight seem; it is thus in keeping with other incidents of the history.

About the same hour on that eventful morning that this extraordinary report was made to the Priests, intelligence of a like startling character broke with like suddenness upon the disciples of Jesus.

Mary of Magdalene came running, breathless with alarm, to Peter and John, telling, in hurried accents, how she and some others had gone out very early, before daybreak, to the sepulchre, taking spices with them to lay out the body of Jesus with more care and decency than the hurried burial on the eve of the Sabbath had allowed, and how, when they came in sight of the tomb, it was open!—the stone was removed! —the tomb had been rifled!—the body was gone!

This last particular, Mary's hasty inference from the fact that the tomb was open, shows that no shadow of a suspicion had crossed her mind that Jesus had risen. Her one engrossing thought was that he was lying dead, the victim of the bitterest hatred; and she rushed to the conclusion that his cruel enemies had pursued him even in death, and violated the sanctity of the grave, not suffering his poor mangled remains to rest in peace where friendly hands had laid them.

At this strange report, Peter and John, followed by Mary, ran to the sepulchre to see if it were indeed so.

Hardly had they gone, when the women, whom Mary had left at the sepulchre, came rushing in, in a transport of wonder and joy, telling that, after she left them, they went into the tomb, and there, to their unutterable amazement, was "*a young man in a long white garment.*" So he appeared to them at first sight. But when he spoke to them, and showed that he knew what they came for, to see the dead body of Jesus, and told them it was not there, that he had risen, and when he bade them go and tell his disciples and Peter that Jesus was living again, they bowed down before him with wonder and great joy, believing him to be no less than an angel from heaven.

Who could this person in "*a long white garment*" be but Jesus, wrapt in his shroud, who, upon becoming aware of the approach of the women, had, after the departure of the guard, retired into the tomb, not being prepared then to make himself known?

That it was he and no other is indicated by one of those slight microscopic particulars that reveal the inimitable hand of truth.*

One of the Gospels states that the women found two angels in the sepulchre. Now if it was Jesus whom they saw and who spoke to them, then he must have taken off the white linen that had been wrapt around his head, and it lay apart, near where his head had rested.

---

* "When there is a detail of many minute particulars, and when to these we apply a close, and, as it may be said, microscopic examination, the contrast between truth and fiction will generally be very striking. Something like this is the difference between the works of nature and art. An artificial flower may be so skilfully made as at first sight to deceive the eye, even of a botanist; but when that and a natural flower are both exposed to the solar microscope, we at once perceive the contrast. The petals of the natural flower, when viewed with the microscope, appear more delicately veined even than when viewed by the naked eye, while those of the artificial flower look like coarse canvas."
—*Miscellaneous Remains from the Commonplace Book of Richard Whately, D.D.* London, 1865.

This white cloth it was, that one or more of the women, with eyes dilated with overwhelming amazement, mistook, in the dim light of the sepulchre, for another angel in white. "Objects imperfectly seen," as Dr. Johnson has remarked, "take form from the imagination."

Had there really been two angels in the sepulchre, would not the one who spoke have spoken for the other and said, "Lo! *we* have told you," and not "Lo! *I* have told you," as is reported?

The first and second Gospels vary but very slightly in their reports of what the person, whom the women found in the sepulchre, said to them. The third Gospel reports him as saying further, "*Remember how he spake unto you when he was yet in Galilee, saying, The Son of man must be delivered into the hands of sinful men and be crucified, and the third day rise again. And they remembered his words.*" As there is nothing in the Gospels that evinces any studied accuracy of statement, that these words are not found in the other Gospels is no decisive evidence that they were not uttered. Suppose the person in the sepulchre was Jesus himself, he might, naturally enough, remind the women of what he had once said. But as he desired them to go away and to go "*quickly,*" and therefore would not be likely to delay them, save by the briefest word or two, my own impression is that, upon being told that Jesus had risen, one or more of the women, before they reached the city, suddenly recollected that Jesus had said that he would rise again, and then when they told his disciples that he had risen, and the startling intelligence was received as an '*idle tale,*' they reminded the disciples of what Jesus had once said, that he would rise again, and, in their hurry and eagerness, they told all in a breath, what the alleged angel said and what they remembered that Jesus had said, mixing the words of the angels that they had heard, and the saying of Jesus that they recollected, so that the latter became mixed up with the former, and all together were understood by some to have been said by the supposed angel.

Upon the departure of the women, Jesus quitted the sepulchre. There was no one there, when, shortly after, Peter and John reached the place.

The women had hardly ended their wonderful story, when Peter and John returned to the city and mournfully reported that they had found it even so as Mary had said: the sepulchre was empty, the body was not there. They had seen no angels. The only strange thing was that the grave-clothes were still there, part in one place, part in another, a circumstance easily accounted for upon the supposition that it was Jesus himself whom the women had seen. He did not put off all the grave-clothes at once, and consequently they were not left lying all together. His body, I imagine, had been placed with his head farthest into the interior of the tomb. When he awoke to life, he divested himself first, as I have just had occasion to note, of the cloth that was wound around his head,* and it lay by itself, apart from the remainder of the shroud, which was not put off until after an interval.

What other clothes Jesus found, we can only

---

* That it was the custom to wind a separate piece of cloth around the head of the dead appears from the account of the Raising of Lazarus, whose face it is said "*was bound about with a napkin.*"

conjecture. The loose, flowing garments of those times needed no special fitting. It may be that the gardener, or some of the persons who had assisted at the burial of Jesus, had provided themselves for that office with garments, which, becoming ceremonially unclean by contact with a dead body, and unfit to be worn on the Sabbath then at hand, were left in the sepulchre or near it. Or, did the watch, in their hasty flight, leave some garments behind them? But this is, perhaps, inquiring too curiously, where all must needs be conjecture.

When Peter and John left the place, they said nothing to Mary. Their silence intimated as plainly as any words that they had found it as she had said. The body was not there.

They left her standing at the entrance of the tomb weeping. She stooped down and looked into it. As Peter and John had been surprised at finding the grave-clothes, part in one place and part in another, so Mary, who had not so near a view of them as they had, caught sight but only dimly, through her tears and the darkness of the sepulchre, of two white objects. They surprised her, but before she had time to make out what they were, there came a voice asking why she wept. Knowing not, for an instant, whence it came, she answered it, but before she finished speaking, she became aware of some one approaching behind her. She turned only partly round, and saw through her tear-bedimmed eyes a man whom she took for the gardener. I think her impression at that instant was, and it was correct, that it was he who had just asked her why she was weeping, for, upon his repeating the question, and not having heard her answer, adding (how naturally!) a further question, "*Whom are you seeking?*" she replied as if she thought that he must have heard what she had just said. She begged him, if he had removed the body, to tell her where it was. Whereupon this person, whom, supposing him to be the gardener, she only glanced at through eyes suffused with tears, called her by name, "Mary!" Then she "turned herself" round,—there was that in the simple utterance of her name that went like lightning to her inmost soul, transporting her out of herself. No voice but one could have so thrilled her whole being. She gazed at him as if she would look him through and through,—the whole life of her in her eyes. It was He! It was the adored Master himself! She gasped out, "Rabboni!" and threw herself at his feet, grasping them in a convulsive, rapturous embrace.

It was not until she returned to the city and heard that the other women had seen, as they declared, two angels in the sepulchre, that, with characteristic precipitancy, she rushed to the confident conclusion that she too had seen those angels, that the two white appearances that she caught sight of when she stooped down and looked into the sepulchre, and did not know what to make of at the time, were those very angels whom the other women had seen, and that they it was who put to her that first question which came she knew not at the moment whence, although at the time she did not dream of their being angels, for she turned her back upon them to talk with a common man. Never would she have done so, had she then thought that there were angels in the sepulchre.

And here I pause over the perfect simplicity, I might almost say, the homeliness, of this most wonderful Event, the Re-appearance of Jesus alive to Mary. There was no sudden apparition, no sudden vanishing. He stood before her in the simple garb of an ordinary man. She saw him before she recognized him. She clasped his knees and knew that it was he, in flesh and blood.

We have seen how, in the case of the guard and of the women, imagination was on the alert to glorify the simplest things and transfigure them with its exaggerating accidents. Mary was as ready as they to become the dupe of the coinage of her brain, as is evident from her rushing to the belief that the white objects that she dimly caught sight of in the sepulchre were angels. Never would she have represented so great a personage as the Messiah was held to be, as returning from the invisible world of the dead in so humble a form that she mistook him for a gardener, had her imagination, quick as it was, had the slightest opportunity to act. Her recognition of him in this lowly garb was too instantaneous, too overwhelming. At the very instant that she was weeping over him as dead, he stands directly before her, calls her by name, and she falls at his feet.

Read any accounts, such as the Roman Catholic Church abounds in, of alleged visions of the Virgin or of this or that saint. Are not those apparitions always arrayed in the glorified costume of preconceived ideas of visitants from the world of spirits, decorated with the symbols of the Church? And thus, in depicting this very event of the Resurrection, Art portrays Christ as ascending from the sepulchre radiating light, and surrounded by clouds of glory. And thus also, were the Gospel narratives pure fabrications, the offspring of the love of the marvellous, would they have represented his Re-appearance alive.

There is a peculiarity in the account of Mary's recognition of Jesus which strikes me as not without significance. I have remarked upon it before. I cannot refrain from a notice of it here. I refer to her exclamation, "Rabboni!" Why was this Hebrew word preserved? It is perfectly translatable, and is immediately translated. There must have been a reason for it. And the reason was, I conceive, that this identical articulation, being the only audible sign of her overpowering transport, bursting involuntarily from her inmost heart, had an emphasis, a world of feeling in it, which no word of a foreign tongue could convey. Any other word would have sounded cold and expressionless, wholly unequal to the occasion. This original exclamation is like the "*Et tu, Brute!*" of Cæsar, which Shakespeare, with the intuition of genius, does not translate.

There are other instances in the Gospels, in which the very words uttered are preserved, and for similar reasons. "*Talitha cumi!*" said Jesus to the child that, at this command, instantly awoke to life. "*Ephphatha!*" was his word in restoring a blind man to sight. These words are immediately translated, but, followed as they were by the most wonderful effects, they sounded in the ears of those present like powerful magical formulas. They had a ring of power which could belong to no other articulations. Those who heard them and witnessed the effects that followed upon their utterance must needs report the identical words that came from the lips of Jesus. So the Apostle Paul uses, more than once, the word "*Abba*," as in Rom. viii, 15, "We have received the spirit of adoption, whereby we cry, *Abba*, Father!" No word of any other language, though it had precisely the same meaning, could have for the Apostle the tender, endearing significance of this brief word in his mother tongue.

Upon recognizing Jesus, Mary, as we have seen, held him by his feet. She clung to them as if she would never let him go; so we may infer from what he is reported to have said to her: "*Touch me not, for I have not yet ascended to my Father; but go to my brothers and tell them I ascend unto my Father and their Father, and to my God and their God.*"

It seems to be thought that there is some mysterious meaning in these words of his, as if they forbade Mary to come near him, or so much as to touch him. But as she afterwards, in all probability, appealed to the fact of having held him by his feet, and as this fact was dwelt upon as proof positive of the sense of touch that it was no spectre that she had seen, but real flesh and blood, may we not surmise that this circumstance has caused what Jesus said to Mary to be reported, not in his exact words, but in the form in which we now have them, and that what he said, and all that he meant to say, was that she was not to stop to embrace him then,—there would be other opportunities of seeing him,—she was to go and tell his brothers that he was still living and about to go to his Father and theirs?

It is not necessary to understand from his manner of expressing himself on this occasion that he intended to say that he was about to go up literally into the sky. It was his purpose to tell, not how he was going, but only that he was about to go to the Father, and he used the popular mode of speaking in which departure from the present state of being is described.

The passage in the fourth Gospel which relates the first appearance of Jesus tells how John outran Peter and waited for him at the sepulchre. This minuteness of detail respecting the movements of Peter and John on that occasion is readily explained when we take the narrative as coming directly from John himself, upon whose mind the slightest incidents of that eventful morning were stamped indelibly. It is not necessary, however, to suppose that he wrote it with his own hand. I do not think that he did. Throughout all the Gospels, the disciples are always spoken of in the third person. This is one great reason why I incline to believe that the Gospels, composed of records previously existing from the earliest time, had for their authors, persons outside of the circle of the immediate disciples of Christ, persons who were either eye and ear witnesses of the things they relate, or obtained their information, as Luke states (Luke i, 1), from "eye-witnesses and ministers of the word." Cultivated writers, like Julius Cæsar, for example, may write about themselves in the third person. But this is an art of literary composition quite beyond such unlettered men as the first disciples were. The opinion which I entertain, for my own satisfaction, concerning the fourth Gospel is, that it is the work of a highly spiritually-minded friend of John's, much younger than he, who held John in the greatest veneration, and obtained from him the materials of this Gospel, not always restricting himself closely to John's communications, but sometimes amplifying them to bring out more fully what he conceived to be their meaning,*

---

* A striking instance of the freedom with which the author of the fourth Gospel introduces his own comments and ampli-

THE STORY OF THE RESURRECTION. 45

but still confining himself substantially to what he received from the venerable Apostle, and very closely in the case of facts, and ending by giving the whole credit of his work to John, not to obtain for it an authority which it would not otherwise possess, but because he felt he had derived it all from his aged friend.

Certain discrepancies with the Story of the first Re-appearance of Christ, as it has now been told, remain to be noticed. They are found in the first Gospel.

While the three other Gospels agree in stating that the stone was removed from the sepulchre before the women reached the place, the first Gospel gives us to understand that the women were present when the stone was rolled away.

The apparent contradiction vanishes when we consider how natural it is, when anything ex-

---

fications may be found in John iii, 11-21, incl. In the immortal chapters of this Gospel, beginning with the fourteenth and ending with the seventeenth, I recognize, not the precise words of Christ, but the inspiration of his Spirit, which, in its expression, is colored and freely amplified in passing through a mind eminently fitted to receive it.

traordinary happens, for the first excited reporters of it, in the eager and hurried state of mind which it causes, to crowd together all the most wonderful particulars without regard to the order of time, so that things are represented as occurring coincidently that occurred successively and at intervals. The story, as it is told in the first Gospel, is an instance of this precipitation. It reads like a first oral report written down. The chief startling incidents are told all at once, in a breath.

Thus viewed, the credibility of what is related to have taken place is not impaired, it is corroborated, as there is undesignedly exhibited the excited state of mind which the extraordinary event related must have produced.

Again. The first Gospel states that Jesus first appeared to all the women who went together to the sepulchre, and who, it says, met him as they were returning to the city. We need have no hesitation in pronouncing this a mistake, since it is easy to see how naturally it was fallen into. As Mary and the women all went together to the sepulchre, and as all but Mary rushed back, declaring that Jesus was alive, and were quickly followed by Mary affirming that she had seen him and held him by his feet, could anything be more natural than that, in the intense excitement of the hour, the impression should be received by some that all the women had seen him and held him by his feet?

In the foregoing exposition of the Accounts of the Re-appearance of Christ alive in the garden where his body had been laid, I am not aware of having had recourse, for the sake of harmonising them, to any forced or far-fetched considerations. I have sought to read them by the light of familiar principles and well-known experiences of our nature.

That the dead body of Christ had disappeared, that a living person was found there, in and near the sepulchre, and that that person was no other than Jesus, I hold to be established by evidence hardly less extraordinary than the great Event itself. It is evidence entirely undesigned, evidence that he was seen by a number of persons without being recognized, and seen by the woman, to whom he made himself known before she recognized him; the evidence, not of men, but of God himself speaking through the natural emotions of the persons present on the spot, all unconsciously on their part. Stronger evidence I can neither desire nor imagine.

Holding the Resurrection of Christ to be an actual fact, must we pronounce it a miracle? A miracle it is in the original sense of the word, which is simply "a wonder." It is a great miracle in this understanding of the term. But was it a miracle in the popular sense? Was it an event out of the established course of nature? As, with all our boasted knowledge, we are acquainted only with the surfaces of things, and cannot pretend to know all the ways of nature, what authority have we for pronouncing it a miracle in the sense of a violation of those ways? Are we not rather bound to conclude that it took place in perfect consistency with the Divine ways, in obedience to some law of nature unknown? And yet not unknown. Has not Christ himself, in the mighty power which he ascribed to Faith in terms the most emphatic, revealed the law, of the operation of which, the marvels that he wrought and his own return to life after death are decisive instances: the law of the supremacy of Spirit over Matter? Accepting this view of the case, we can hardly fail to see that all the ado that has been made about miracles is out of place. On that score, we have afflicted our souls in vain.

Living, dying, and rising from the dead in profoundest harmony with the Divine Will and order, through a faith, identified with his inmost personal consciousness, in the Infinite One dwelling in him, and in all things, animate and inanimate, Christ is our fullest Revelation of God, and of the Divine life in the soul of man.

His Resurrection was justified by the power with which it wrought. To change those poor men, who first put faith in him, into saints and martyrs, through whom the world was to be revolutionised, it was worth while for the greatest of the sons of men to awake from the deep slumber of death, and show himself to them and inspire them with a faith in things unseen such as was never felt before. Had he not done so, his memory would have faded away from the world into an insubstantial dream of the Past, casting no light of sanctity upon the Present, nor of hope upon the Future. His disciples would have gone mourning back to their boats and nets on the Sea of Galilee. But as it was, assured beyond the shadow of a misgiving that he who had been all in all to them, for whom they had forsaken all else, was still living, with a courage that princes and all the powers of Church and State could not daunt, those humble men went forth and published their faith in the Risen Christ, sealing that faith with their blood. This was the one Fact, upon the truth of which they staked life and all that makes life dear: that Christ had risen from the dead, and was still living. "If," said the Pharisee, who was early converted to their faith, and who became the foremost of them, "if thou shalt confess with thy mouth," that is, speak boldly out and at the peril of thy life avow thy faith in Christ as a man from God, "and shalt believe in thine heart that God hath raised him from the dead, thou shalt be saved,"—saved from the fear of man and the fear of death. And this is salvation in the fullest sense of the word.

But it was not only at the first, in one generation only, that the fact of the Resurrection of Christ was of this vital importance. Its power was not then exhausted. Never has it been of deeper interest than at this hour, when Science has become invested, in the popular mind, with extraordinary authority, and would fain bring the world to the worship of matter and unconscious physical force. Thank Heaven for him who appeared in all the might of the Spirit, for "the power of his Resurrection," the crowning evidence of the supremacy of mind over matter!

REMARKS

UPON

THE CHARACTER OF CHRIST

AND

THE HISTORICAL CLAIMS OF THE FOUR GOSPELS.

REMARKS.

In the preceding pages I have told again the Story of the First Re-appearance of Christ after death. I do not know that the same view of it has ever been taken by any one else. I have no expectation that it will meet with any extensive acceptance. It is the exceeding interest of the Story that has moved me to this repetition. I am betraying perhaps the infirmity of Age. As in our first childhood we love to hear, so in our second, we love to tell, the same stories over and over again.

THE DECLINE OF FAITH.

If, in regard to studies of this class, there is, among the liberally disposed, one characteristic of the present time more marked than another, it is the Decline of Faith, not only in the great Christian fact of the Resurrection of Christ, but in the historical authority of the Gospels altogether.

Theodore Parker—all honor to his memory!—said long ago in his first and chief work, "A Discourse of Religion," a work that has had great influence in setting the present fashion of thinking, that we have no warrant for the truth of any incident related in the Gospels beyond the fact that Jesus was persecuted and suffered a violent death, which, although Mr Parker says it lay in the nature of the case, would now in these sceptical times, I suspect, be called in question, were there not on record the explicit testimony of the Roman historian to the crucifixion of Christ.

That faith in historical Christianity is on the decline among us needs no special proof. The fact is patent. It is in all the air. The appearance of a denomination called Free Religionists is evidence sufficient. Those, who are ranked under this title, are understood to relinquish the Christian name, and to hold that, for the superiority claimed for Christianity over all other religions, there is no historical foundation, that it has the same legendary origin with the other religions that have sprung up in the far East. As historical records, the Gospels are accounted of very little value. Having thus fallen, historically, into disrepute, regarded as collections of mere fables or myths, they are ceasing to be studied, or even referred to, apart from their moral precepts, with any particular interest.

As such ways of thinking are becoming common, I cannot but see and lament that the true character and contents of these Writings are very imperfectly understood. Even Mr Parker, who pronounced so decisively upon their credibility, does not seem to have given them any thorough study. Why should he, if he believed them to be fables? In the work already referred to, he says that Christ taught the reprobation of the majority of mankind, and, in proof thereof, refers to the passage in the Sermon on the Mount, which says that "broad is the way that leads to destruction, etc.," a simple picture of human life, not first given by Christ, equivalent to, "Folly leads to ruin and has her thousands to follow her, while the way of Wisdom is narrow, and only the few pursue it," a saying all but proverbial. Again, Mr Parker objects, if my memory serves me, that Christ promised his disciples, when they should be arraigned before magistrates, miraculous assistance. The language of Christ does not necessarily bear any such construction. He simply assured them, that, when they found themselves in that position, *it would be given them,*—a form of speaking synonymous with, *they would be able,*—to speak and bear themselves as they should; with the occasion would come the true spirit to meet it. Once, some time before his death, my venerated friend, Waldo Emerson, was telling me of the fidelity of a man who had been long in his service. I quoted, partly to myself, "*Whosoever would be great, let him serve.*" "Who said that?" exclaimed my friend: "say it again." While he betrayed his lack of familiarity with the New Testament, he was struck, as he well might be, with the wisdom of a saying that fell from the lips of Jesus by the wayside, in familiar intercourse with a little company of poor fishermen; a saying identical with that, but of far deeper significance, which the father of modern philosophy is renowned for announcing from his library: "To command Nature, you must obey her." The comparison, by the way, suggests the contrast. How great the difference between the two! The poor peasant of Judea exemplified in life and in death the grander truth that he uttered. The philosopher, with all his learning, failed, in the lower domain of physical science, to be true to his own precept.

To return. It seems to me sometimes as if to the wisest and most enlightened the Gospels are sealed books. How indeed can it be otherwise? For long years they have been read diligently enough, Heaven knows! but always by the light of the theological systems, in the interest of which they have been interpreted so long that it is all but impossible to dissociate their phraseology from the dogmatic "hoar of ages" which cleaves to it.

When here among us, in New England, the heavy fetters of the old theology began to fall away, and a freer mode of thinking to prevail, it was the aim of the liberal denominations to relieve the Scriptures from orthodox interpretations and to show that they give no countenance to the old dogmas, to declare, in fine, what they do not mean rather than what they do. Consequently those who forsook the old faith, could only tell what they did not believe. Beyond that, we had no positive, clearly-defined faith; and so, in the eyes of many, there was but little difference to see to, between the non-orthodox and downright unbelievers.

I suppose that, in the progress of thought, this state of things had to be. But a consequence of it is, that, as the Gospels were no longer believed to be preternaturally inspired, or to sanction the old doctrines, they ceased to be studied with particular interest. It was enough that they were found to be not Calvinistic documents.

THE EFFECT OF A MISTAKEN THEOLOGY.

Furthermore, and here is a fact that demands most serious attention: Our Christian Theology stands insurmountably in the way of a due appreciation of the historical character of the Gospels.

It is held by all denominations of Christians, orthodox and liberal, without exception, as a fundamental article of the Christian Faith, that the Revelation contained in the Gospels is pre-

THE EFFECT OF A MISTAKEN THEOLOGY. 61

ternatural, and that only as they are so regarded have they any special authority, it being affirmed as a first principle of our Theology that only by miracles, that is, only by suspensions of the established laws of nature, can a Revelation be proved to come from God.

Now if he, of whom the Gospels tell us, has really brought to mankind a Divine Revelation, then must all that he said and did be of supreme interest to all who are seeking to learn the Divine ways. A Revelation from the Author of all things must harmonize with and illumine all else that has come from the same Source, and prove our greatest guiding light in the study of nature. What is the end and aim of natural science but the discovery of the Ultimate Power, a seeking after God through the study of his ways?

But when Christ is represented, in his being, or only in his working, as above nature, he is put outside of nature, and consequently outside of the sphere of scientific inquiry. And it may be said, as it has been said by the most eminent student of nature in our day, that Science has nothing to do with him. Accordingly, left to itself, what else is to be expected but just what we see: Science making, indeed, wonderful discoveries and inventions, employing forces of the nature of which it has no idea, but finding nothing to believe in, nothing to appeal to our deepest sentiments but unintelligent, unconscious matter and blind physical force?

It is no wonder that our scientific inquirers, searching in the dark among atoms and monads, and I know not what creations of the scientific imagination, after the Ultimate Cause, can find no Creative Intelligent Power present in the Universe. Laborious and acute as they are, what else can they do, since they get no help from the great light that would guide their investigations? Sad is it to find that "star-eyed Science" returns from ranging through the Universe to bring us back "a message of despair." It has, however, this great excuse for the poverty of its results: it has been warned off from the quarter whence the guiding light comes. The advocates of Christianity, insisting upon a representation of Christ that puts him beyond the range of inquiry, have virtually forbidden Science to look for aid in this direction. A

THE EFFECT OF A MISTAKEN THEOLOGY. 63

false theology it is, I repeat, that is responsible for the materialistic modes of thought now so prevalent.

Supernatural Christ was, taking this word as synonymous with superphysical, but when he is represented as working preternaturally, he is not only outside of the range of Science, but beyond the reach of rational belief. If his works are outside of the natural order of things, how are they to be distinguished from creations of the human imagination, since the demonstration of the truth of any fact consists in its being shown to be, actually or presumably, in harmony with all else that is known to be true? *Omne verum consonat vero.*

As far as the eye has penetrated, there everywhere reigns throughout the Universe a consummate order, which is one grand characteristic of the Creator. The laws of nature, that we talk about, what are they but the Divine ways under another name? To affirm of any event that it is an interruption of the laws of nature is the same as saying that God contradicts himself, which is incredible.

Here we are confronted with the chief obstacle to the recognition and treatment of the Gospels as genuine histories. By the insistence of those who profess to believe them, they abound in accounts of so-called miracles.

In an earlier publication, "Jesus and his Biographers" (1838), taking for granted the universally received theology, I assumed that the miracles were actual suspensions of the laws of nature, and that Christ was specially gifted with preternatural power for the express purpose of proving his Divine authority. And what I chiefly sought to do was to show how fully in accordance with the dignity of his personal character and with the simplicity of nature he is represented as using his peculiar gift.

I have since been led to the conclusion that the alleged miracles were not miracles in the commonly received sense of the word, but extraordinary natural facts, and that there is no reason nor necessity for supposing that Christ had any power to suspend the action of the laws of nature. I find nothing in the Gospels that authorises this supposition.

The definition of a miracle as a suspension of the laws of nature is of modern origin, unknown

THE EFFECT OF A MISTAKEN THEOLOGY.

to the Scriptures, both Old and New, which I found I had, with all the world, been reading from a mistaken point of view, a point of view based upon the mechanical theory of nature, an offspring of modern Science. Nature being conceived of as a vast mechanism, whatever appears to be a departure from its settled order is to be pronounced a miracle, a break in the natural course of things. Such is the common belief.

Not so, not so, did the authors of the Bible look upon the world. The Hebrew word, and the Greek word also, translated in our Scriptures "miracle," means simply "sign" or "prodigy," and all that our English word "miracle" signifies, in its etymological sense, is "a wonder."

The writers of the Bible saw everywhere, not the working of blind physical forces, but intelligent, spiritual agencies. It was God who did all things, directly, or through the ministry of angels or demons. Such is the Bible view of the economy of the world, with which there were no signs or wonders that were not in harmony, and of which they were not a part.

Moreover, in respect of the alleged miracles

in the New Testament, I do not find that Jesus ever claimed any preternatural power. He affirmed, indeed, that the wonders that were witnessed were wrought by God, but as emphatically did he declare that they were wrought through faith, a natural, spiritual, God-given force, planted deep in human nature.

The view of the miracles, therefore, which, after all these years, I have come finally to rest in, is, that, marvels as they are, they were facts as natural as the rising and shining of the sun; and, indeed, of all facts, the most natural, since they occurred in obedience to the highest, or deepest, law of nature, the law of the supremacy of Spirit.

Were this view of the so-called miraculous relations accepted, the air of incredibility which now invests the Gospels would disappear, and their claim to be treated no longer as fables, but as possibly true histories, would be seen to be not wholly groundless.

And not only so, upon a careful and candid examination of their contents, it might be discovered that the so-called miracles which they relate, instead of being suspensions of natural laws, are revelations thereof, revelations, in fact, of the very highest of the laws of Nature, the law of the Supremacy of mind over matter. Then, in direct opposition to the representations of Materialism, Christ would be seen to be the Revealer of Spirit, of an immaterial Power as the creative, all-animating Cause and Soul of the physical world. No longer should we find ourselves cabined, cribbed, confined in the midst of a vast machine, worked by brute forces that sweep us away like dust, but in the mansion of an Infinite Spirit of Life, of Wisdom, and of Love, and in as many as are led by the Spirit we should behold beings partaking of the Supreme nature, and of whose high position and destiny their lofty powers and graces would be more significant than the white robes and wings of angels.

As I have just said, Christ never pretended to possess any preternatural gift. That his was a finely organized nature, that he was inspired by a peerless religious genius, and was endowed with a keen and searching moral insight, the most orthodox, whatever else and more they believe him to be, will not question. ("Perfect man" as well as "perfect God" is the language of the old creed.) While he differed from all other men greatly, the difference was not in kind, but in degree. He was no other wise made than all men are. Of all human beings, he was the most human. In him the greatest and best in our nature was most fully developed.

It is, then, in the completeness of his nature as a human being, not in any superaddition thereto, that his Godlikeness is shown, his Divine Sonship. In all the good of every age, in every good deed, we have hints, more or less significant, of the same sacred relationship to the Highest. But in Christ shines the great Revelation, full-orbed, the sun amidst the lesser lights of the firmament. High beyond all stands that wondrous Hebrew youth. In him we have the fullest vision of the Infinite Spirit, the Father. Through him also we behold in all men, by virtue of the nature which they share with him, children of God,—rebellious, lost, children, but still children of God.

This Idea of Christ, bringing him within the

embrace of our most sacred sympathies, of our faith and our veneration, creates a new faith in the transcendent possibilities of our nature. Does it not give us, for example, a new sense of the height to which man may rise above Self, as we contemplate Jesus, in the midst of multitudes rending the air with their acclamations, and behold him working the greatest marvels, as if, so far as he was concerned, they were the commonest human offices, seeing in them no glory of his own, but only the glory of God in the power of Faith?

As he was one with all nature, all nature bears witness to him, and is, in return, illumined and consecrated by the light that radiates from him up to the throne of God and down to the humblest of mankind, to the meanest creature that breathes.

If we are ever to have a true philosophy of the Universe and of man's position therein, Christ must be the corner-stone thereof. It cannot be that such a revelation as he is of the Greatest and Best will not shed light far and wide over the whole sphere of human knowledge, since the Universe, seen and unseen, is One. Even upon the old orthodox ideas of the Christian Revelation, it has its theology, or philosophy of the world. But what a philosophy! Not the light of the knowledge of the glory of God shining into the heart from the person of Christ, but a theology that shows us the Universe reddened by the glare of an ever-burning hell, into which, age after age, are driven by Almighty Wrath, for the sin of their first progenitor, myriads of human souls: a sight which high orthodox authorities have taught, enhances the bliss of the saints in heaven.

THE MYTHICAL THEORY.

In addition to erroneous views of the nature of Christ and of the marvels related in the Gospels, the mythical theory of their origin, with which Strauss has made us familiar, has helped to undermine the faith of many in the historical claims of these Writings. That theory has been accepted as fully accounting for their existence.

Strauss does not appear to have taken care to ascertain the real meaning of the Gospels before applying his theory to them. Like all those who deny their historical character, he argues, not against the most rational construction of which they admit, but against the commonly received mistaken interpretations of them. It was obviously for the interest of his theory, as it is of all theories unfavorable to their historical claims, that they should be made to appear as improbable as possible.

THE DATE OF THE GOSPELS.

The difficulty of determining the date of the Gospels—the fact that, as scholars affirm, there is no historical evidence of their existence before the second century—has, doubtless, gone far to create unbelief in their value as histories.

I am at a loss to understand why so much stress is laid upon the external argument for their truth. Unquestionably, it would be interesting to know when precisely and by whom they were written; and were it proved that they were written by the persons whose names they bear, it would help to confirm our faith in them. But even if we had the most satisfactory external evidence on this point, there would still remain the question whether their authors were not, more or less, mistaken. And this question would depend for settlement upon their intrinsic character and upon no extrinsic considerations. In determining what they are, whether legends or true narratives, it is not necessary that we should know when or by whom they were written. They are to be interrogated. They must speak for themselves. A lapidary does not need to know the history of a diamond in order to decide whether it be a diamond or not.

Admitting that there is no historical evidence of their having been in existence before the second century, nevertheless, since in all ages men are prompted, as by an irresistible instinct, to express and perpetuate the impression which events at all remarkable make on them, it is, under the circumstances, very unlikely, to say the least, that nothing was put in a written form about Christ until a hundred years after his time.

We must not forget the vast revolution which the Printing Press has made in the means of publication. In that old time, the manufacture and multiplication of copies of a written work must have proceeded very slowly, and it may have been in existence for a considerable period before it became so multiplied and so widely known as to be said, properly speaking, to be published. Publication now is the work of a day. Then it was the work of years.

Such being the case, that the Gospels are not mentioned by any writer before the second century does not preclude the possibility of their being compilations of written narratives that came into existence and had been passing from hand to hand and slowly multiplied long before. The third Gospel (Luke i, 1) states that there were "many" such in circulation before that was written.

That the Gospels really are of this description, mostly compiled of narratives that were in existence at a very early period, is, to my mind, abundantly clear from their internal character. Even considered as legends, they show by their lack of connection, by the difficulty of reducing them to a continuous narrative or to any satisfactory order of time, that they are composed of different pieces put together with no particular care.

That they are not mere legends, however, or,

if legendary, only so in a few passages, the whole tenor, of the first three Gospels especially, shows. They bear numerous, inimitable marks of being true histories; and not only so, but of histories that existed, in some form or other, wellnigh contemporaneously with the events narrated. They have all the freshness of first reports. They are warm with the life and with the impress of the facts which they relate. So strongly do I find them thus marked, that, for my own part, I need no external evidence to reinforce their credibility. Like all true things, they are their own credentials.

Alexander the Great, at the tomb of Achilles, wished that he might have such a herald of his exploits as that hero had in Homer. Wisely has it been said, "Do great deeds and they will sing themselves."* Great things, said and done, strike all who hear and behold them, and hearers and beholders there always are, who must publish what they have heard and seen, or die. They are driven by the overpowering force of truth and nature, the inspiration of God,

---

* Emerson.

to proclaim it in all possible ways. This is what is meant by great deeds singing themselves.

And this is what the Gospels are most striking instances of. The incidents of the life of Jesus could no more fail to be told by every means then known than the sun could fail to give light. Written reports of them did not wait to appear till there was a demand for them. They created the demand. As I have paused over the different scenes of that wonderful Life, and have been touched to the heart by the God-like bearing, at once so original and so natural, of this Man of men, it has seemed to me that, if men had held their peace, the very stones in the streets, over which walked those blessed feet, would have cried aloud. But men did not hold their peace. They could not. And consequently, by word of mouth and by written words as well, the world instantly began to ring with the immortal Story.

FAMILIARITY WITH THE BIBLE.

In addition to the causes, which I have mentioned, of the Decline of Faith in our Christian Records, there remains one to be briefly noticed. We are all conscious of its effect. A common proverb states it. Familiarity with the Bible has bred, not contempt, but indifference and despair of ever finding it interesting. It has fared with it as Hamlet's soliloquy fared with Charles Lamb. He had heard that piece of Shakespeare so often from the mouths of declamatory boys and men, that he could not tell, he said, whether it is good, bad, or indifferent. Put into our hands when we were too young to understand them, the Scriptures must needs have become wearisome, associated perhaps with the hard labor of learning to read. We have been required to con them verse by verse, chapter by chapter, as a religious task, sometimes as a punishment, for mischief or filial disobedience. We have got them by heart, but only the words, to which, regardless of their meaning, we have attached a superstitious sanctity. How irksome it has all been, who is not ready to confess? Who has not wished that he could read the Bible now for the first time? Old Thomas Fuller, pious man that he was, able to draw spiritual nourishment from the genealogies, and even perhaps, I should not wonder, "from the unedifying tenth of Nehemiah," betrays his weariness of this Bible-reading routine, when he tells us how his conscience pricked him, as he caught himself turning over the leaf to see whether the daily chapter that he was bound to read was long.

THE GREAT LOSS.

And yet, after all, the Gospels have been studied and commented upon, letter by letter, laboriously enough. How vast the literature they have created! The hundred and sixty miles of shelves in the British Museum could hardly contain the volumes that have been written about them.

But all this labor has been spent, as I have said, mainly in the interest of this or that system of theology, and all upon the fatal assumption that these writings are the history of a Life out of the natural order of things. The consequence is that, as the old theology is shorn of its prestige, and the general mind is becoming familiarised with the universality of law, all faith in the historical truth of Christianity is going to decay.

THE GREAT LOSS.

This faith destroyed,—what does it import? Nothing less than this: the loss of the noblest Realised Ideal of human nature that has ever yet appeared in the history of mankind, a loss we can poorly afford to bear, especially, now when Science, with its powerful instruments, revealing to us the awful mystery of Being, and crushing us under a sense of our apparent insignificance, in the pride of her dazzling triumphs, is making popular speculations that are at war, I say not, with Christianity, but with all but "the ghost" of a Religion.* In losing Christ,

---

* "He tried to give her yet another idea of the size of the Universe. . . . 'There is a size at which dignity begins,' he exclaimed: 'further on, there is a size at which grandeur begins; further on, there is a size at which solemnity begins; further on, a size at which awfulness begins; further on, a size at which ghastliness begins. That size faintly approaches the size of the stellar universe. So am I not right in saying that those who exert their imaginative powers to bury themselves in the depths of that universe merely strain their faculties to gain a new horror? . . . If you are cheerful, and wish to remain so, leave the study of astronomy alone. Of all sciences, it alone deserves the character of the terrible. Then, if, on the other hand, you are restless, worried by your worldly affairs, and anxious about the future, study astronomy

we lose a priceless pledge of the transcendent powers and destiny of human nature, an all-comforting, all-inspiring Revelation of the Sonship of man, of the Fatherhood of God, and a great light is extinguished whereby Science might be led from the downward path which it is pursuing up to the life and power of Spirit. This is the unspeakable pity of it.

It cannot be too deeply impressed upon our minds that it is not the teachings of Christ, taken apart from him, but it is he himself, his perfected personal being, that is the great Revelation, the essential life and power of Christianity. "The highest cannot be expressed in words," but only in Life. Life is the language in which God communicates with man.

---

at once. Your troubles will be reduced amazingly. But your study will reduce them in a singular way,—by reducing the importance of everything. So that the science is still terrible even as a panacea.' "—(*Two in a Tower. A Novel, by Thomas Hardy.*) IF ANY MAN BE IN CHRIST, THERE IS A NEW CREATION. With Christ in the heart, with the faith in God and man that rests on him as on a Rock, the dread Mystery may be affronted with unshaken faith and triumphant hope.

Happy he who translates it into his own life, be his creed what it may!

What exalts Christ, to my mind, high above all other great leaders of mankind, and deepens inexpressibly my sense of his most original personal greatness, is the fact that, not only was he far greater than his word, great as his word was, and of what other can this be said? but that, so far as human sympathy was concerned, he lived and died Alone, Alone with God.

Other great leaders have very soon gathered around themselves a greater or less number of adherents, who have caught their spirit, appreciated their aims, entered into their work, and, continuing faithful to the end, have been to them a world of encouragement and support. But, from the first to the last, Christ had not a soul on earth that understood his purpose.

The little company of ignorant men who attended him were drawn to him with a force of which neither he nor they were conscious, by his commanding personal qualities expressed in his whole bearing, in every glance of his eye, beaming with kindness, or flashing with indignation, in every accent of his voice, thrilling them with its tone of perfect sincerity. But they were following him with very mercenary views. They were depending upon his making them princes in Israel. The more they felt the power of his character, the more they trusted in him, and the more confident were they that he would fulfil their expectations. The kingdom which they implicitly believed that he would establish was a kingdom of national wealth and splendor. But as to what filled his whole heart, and for which he lived and was to die, they were, as he more than once called them, children. In that regard they were as ignorant as the dumb brute that follows its master. In his extremest agony they fell asleep. And when at last the crisis came, and an awful death confronted him, they fled and left him alone with the grim horror.

Not only was he thus without a friend, who, entering into his mind, and understanding his high purpose, could lighten his burden by sharing it, but he was beset at every step by mortal foes, who, urged by bigotry and hate, were bent upon his destruction, accounting it a God-service.

And he, who thus lived and died, solitary and alone among men, to whom he yearned with a brother's heart, was not a person of an austere temperament, such as would be best able to endure so lonely a lot. He was distinguished for his tenderness. It is evident from the style of his discourse that he cherished companionship with Nature in its various forms, with the birds of the air and the flowers of the field. So gentle-natured was he that Art, in its endeavor to portray him, overlooks his extraordinary strength of character, and depicts him as a person of feminine softness. Oh no, there was nothing repellent in his appearance. When those around him would fain drive children away as intruders into his presence, he was much displeased; he called the children to him, took them in his arms and pronounced his immortal benediction upon childhood. And children it was who welcomed him to the great city with their shrill hosannas. Women sat at his feet, ministered to his wants, and poured their fragrant ointments on his person in token of their reverence, and one wretched creature fell at his feet and covered them with her kisses, and bathed them with her tears and wiped them with her hair.

With a heart ever open to all human sorrows and going in his youth straight to a baptism of blood, with no friend in sympathy with what was dearest to him, how profound was the solitude of the soul in which he lived and died! What elevation of mind, nothing less than sublime, does it betoken, that, in the absence of all human sympathy, he bore himself with a fraternal consideration for others and a forgetfulness of himself as habitual and as perfect as if life was for him, from first to last, a triumphal progress, attended at every step by the welcoming acclamations of a world! Who shall fathom the great deep of his Faith, of his faith in God, of his faith in man? Only once, for a passing moment, in his sharpest agony, did his mind misgive him. He might well have feared that he was the dupe of a delusion, that there was no God in heaven to have pity on him, that all truth and virtue had fled the earth, when he stood before Pilate, forsaken by every friend, with the demoniac yell, "Crucify him! Crucify him!" ringing in his ears, and all that the world accounted respectable and religious arrayed against him. "Art thou a king?" asked his judge. "Thou sayest it," he replied, "I am a King. For this end I was born, and for this cause came I into the world, to bear witness to the truth; and every true man hearkens to my voice." Let the darkness, hiding from him both heaven and earth, gather around him as thickly as it might, it could not shake his faith in Truth and in the existence and loyalty of good men and true.

In contrast with Christ, how poor is the outcome of our vaunted superior enlightenment! How poverty-stricken looks our boasted Science in the appearance, among our so-called most advanced thinkers, of a denomination professing as its distinction, in relation to questions of the deepest interest, an utter inability to affirm or to deny! We are measuring the heights, sounding the depths, of the material Universe, and reducing its mightiest forces to our daily service, but around the Divine in Nature and in the human soul, clouds and darkness, exhaled from the broad fields of our Science, are gathering thick and fast.

Jesus, alone, and in an ignorant age, affirmed the Fatherhood of God and the Sonship of man. He lived and died, resting in immovable faith on these affirmations. And their truth?—behold the God-given warrant of it in the peerless character which they fashioned, and in the life which has gone forth therefrom through generations and is still, in countless unacknowledged ways, re-creating the world. Where is the wise? Where is the scribe? Where is the disputer of the present age to answer our deepest questions? Is not God again making foolish the wisdom of this world? Why should we care for protoplasms and molecules, if all is to end in the annihilation of God and of man?

"I'd rather be
A Pagan suckled in a creed outworn"

than have the whole world of things laid bare to me in the light of Science, only to find at last that there is no God in heaven, and no hope for man on this earth, groaning and travailing together in pain as it is.

The result of what has now been said of Christ, the reason why we cannot afford to lose him, but must cherish him as our dearest treasure, as the cardinal fact in human history, is briefly this: His character, being the creation of a theory of human nature, if you please so to call it, I prefer to say, of an Ideal, which represents man as standing in a relation to the Highest, best symbolized, though inadequately, by that of a child to a father,—this Realized Ideal in Christ, appealing directly as it does to the most powerful sentiments of our nature, is an all-sufficient witness to the truth of this Ideal. He was no preternatural apparition. He was no myth. He was a Solid Fact, at once human and divine, in the fullest harmony with the Divine order of the world, a living demonstration of the Sonship of man and the Fatherhood of God.

CHRIST FROM A LEGENDARY POINT OF VIEW.

Far otherwise than what I have now represented him must he be conceived of when the accounts of him that have come down to us are treated as mere fables that had their origin years after his time. Then he appears, as M. Renan says he appeared to him before he went to Syria, as a dim personage of doubtful existence. No longer revered as the creative centre of all that is good and hopeful in our modern life, to be cherished with the deepest reverence and the liveliest faith, he becomes a vague vision which we must take care that we do not unduly magnify, as he is held responsible for all the errors, and they are many and great, of which he has been the innocent occasion, and which have claimed the authority of his name. As well, by the way, may the magnificent spectacle of Creation that lies all around us be charged with the monstrous superstitions engendered by the ignorance and fear with which it has been contemplated.

Although regarded as a legendary personage, he yet may be acknowledged as an eminent moral teacher. But apart from him, his sayings might as well have come down to us anonymously for any peculiar power they possess. It is a mistake, I conceive, to magnify him merely as a moral Instructor, as if this were his chief claim upon our reverence. The Man was a great deal greater than the Speaker. No sounds of the lips, though such as angels use, could express the unsearchable riches of his faith and truth. It is his personal character, not any novelty of doctrine, but his very life, poured into every word and work, that has made him great among men beyond compare. He dealt in no hearsays, spoke from no external dictation, but from the profound convictions of his own soul, upon which he planted himself as a king upon his throne, making a crown of thorns outshine all earthly diadems, and "the world come round to him." If the words of Luther were half battles, the words of Christ were victories. In fine, it is the unrivalled force of his character, the divine humanity of his life, God within him, that clothes him with an authority before which "the human soul of universal earth" must bow in veneration and love.

THE GOSPELS, HOW TO BE APPROACHED.

It is difficult, I know, to approach the Gospels unbiassed by any theories of belief or unbelief whatever. We look to find in them the confirmation of our preconceived ideas; and what we seek we are pretty sure to find. It is, indeed, quite impossible to read them without some hypothesis, more or less pronounced, of their character and contents, nor is it desirable. In the pursuit of truth in any department of inquiry, previous

THE GOSPELS, HOW TO BE APPROACHED.

suppositions, or divinations, are indispensable. We must have some thread to string our facts upon, some idea to verify. Only we must be on our guard and take great care that our theories do not run away with us, as they are very apt to do, out of sight of everything that contradicts them.

My own supposition, suggested by certain obvious characteristics of these Writings, is simply this: They are neither theological documents nor fabulous compositions, but, substantially, genuine histories, not perfect (what history is?), but accounts of things that were actually said and done.

Accordingly, what I have endeavored to keep in view as my sole aim has been to ascertain how much there is in them, which, being consistent in itself, with all the actual and probable circumstances of the case, and with all that is known to be true, carries in itself the evidence of its truth.

That no bias of preconceived notions has impaired the singleness of my purpose, I cannot pretend. It is quite impossible to project one's self out of the sphere of inherited modes of thought, and, without going too far, take the right stand beyond the reach of their influence. I have done what I could to read the Gospels as if they were just put into my hands, excluding from view the peculiar theological and official representations of him whose acts and sayings they record.

As they abound in references to times, places, and persons, and are obviously and eminently circumstantial, that a faithful and candid examination will make it appear, beyond all question, whether they are true or fabulous, or, if a mixture of both, to what extent, I have no doubt.

This confidence has been amply repaid by signs and marks of an unmistakable significance, which have disclosed themselves at every step. I make no boastful claim. But I am free to say that many of the inimitable undesigned evidences of truth and nature, which I have indicated from time to time in the Gospel narratives, have never that I know of been observed before. They would have been found long ago, I doubt not, had they been looked for. Erroneous ideas of the character of the Gospels, and of him of whom they tell, have prevented a search in the direction that would have led to the discovery of these internal evidences of their truth.

That these internal evidences have been so long overlooked,—does it not show how truly undesigned they were? Had they been intended to create an air of truth, they would have been made more conspicuous.

That I have in no instance mistaken fancies for facts, I cannot venture to affirm. Wherever I may have done so, a keener critical faculty than I possess will make it manifest. I am far from thinking that I have left nothing undiscovered in this most interesting field of inquiry. I have hardly gone beyond its borders, but I have gone far enough to be convinced of its inexhaustible richness.

THE GOSPELS READ BETWEEN THE LINES.

I have said more than once, in previous publications, that, in order to be rightly understood, the Gospels must be read between the lines. In truth they have already been read a great deal in this way; and the diverse interlineal meanings that they are made to yield, who can number? But they have been thus read mostly by the highly colored light of theological dogmas and metaphysical systems founded upon misinterpretations of the written word. I have endeavored to discover what is legible between the lines by the pure, white light of the undisputed truth of nature. What I have thus read, I submit to the judgment of the reader in the following instances.

The Baptism of Jesus.

I begin with a passage that I have dwelt upon often before, the passage that relates to the Baptism of Jesus.

It impresses me deeply, in the first place, because I find that it is an account of a great moment, of an era indeed, in his spiritual development; and then because of the perfect truth to nature, to the laws of the human mind, with which the experience which he then had is described.

When it is stated (in the second Gospel) that, after his baptism, "*immediately the Spirit driveth him into the wilderness,*" I read between the lines that his baptism was no cold formality, but that he was so profoundly moved by it that he could not rest in his old familiar relations. Up to that hour he had lived his ordinary retired life, cherishing in the secrecy of his own bosom his high aspirations, meditating the work to which he felt himself ever more and more urgently called. How thoroughly acquainted he was with the spirit of the time, with the corruption and savage bigotry of the ruling classes especially, his subsequent utterances abundantly attest. Consequently he saw with ever-growing clearness that it would be certain death if he dared to obey the inward call, and go forth and faithfully declare the truth concerning God and man then buried out of sight under formalities and traditions which were hardening the heart and perverting the conscience.

At last the hour came when he could delay no longer. He must obey the sacred impulse of the Spirit. A time of great religious excitement was causing multitudes from far and wide to flock to the Voice and the Baptism in the Desert on the banks of the Jordan. Jesus quitted his home and went with the throng, deliberately and formally, to be cleansed of all hesitation and delay, and to devote himself to a work that had but one end, a violent death.

It was his first public step, the step that costs,

an act by which he virtually pronounced sentence of death on himself. With this devotion of himself to the Supreme Will when it willed for him so appalling a fate, there came a new and overpowering consciousness of the ineffable blessedness of a perfect unity with the Highest and Best. So new and deep was this experience that he could not rest in his old surroundings. He must flee, driven from within, by the Spirit, to the silence and solitude of the Desert, there to ponder his exalted relationship, which was now impressed upon him as never before, and prepare himself for the fatal career in which he had now taken the first irrevocable step.

Now, as never before, and as it never could have been until he "converted conviction into act," his faith was deepened beyond the possibility of being shaken or disobeyed. In the deep peace that overflowed his soul, he had the witness of the Spirit of the Most High that it was no hallucination, but the voice of God in his heart, that he was obeying.

Bearing in mind this faith which now knew no misgiving, and the power of which his fleeing to the Wilderness reveals, and considering also how natural it is for the boldest figures of the imagination, in moments of intense excitement, to rise before the mind as representative of the emotion that overpowers us, we cannot fail to see how true it is to nature that Jesus should describe that new and beatific consciousness of oneness with the All-Perfect as a vision of heaven, as heaven thrown open to him. "The moment," says Emerson, "our discourse is inflamed with passion or exalted by thought, it clothes itself in images."

And is it not with equal truth to nature that a dove, the common symbol of love and peace, happening to hover within the rapt vision of Jesus, as he came up out of the water, " in bodily shape" only an ordinary dove, was instantly glorified by his raised imagination, and transfigured into a heaven-sent messenger? What is more common, in moments of deep emotion, than for the most familiar incidents and appearances to be invested with the significance of omens or portents?

And is it not in accordance with no uncommon experience that the words of ancient Scripture, " *Thou art my beloved Son, in whom I am well pleased,*" coming suddenly, involuntarily, to the mind of Jesus as expressive of his newborn consciousness of the approbation of the Highest, should seem to him as though sounded in his ears by an articulate voice, and should be so described?

Does this interpretation of the Baptism of Jesus, which I read, in the very handwriting of truth and nature, between the lines, seem strained? Ah! if we had ever had an experience in the remotest degree akin to his at that great moment, these figures of the imagination would be felt to be all inadequate to describe his unutterable peace of mind, the natural accompaniment and consequence of the divine consciousness then created within him.

In the Desert.

In the account of what passed in the Wilderness in those temptations with which he contended, and which, according to the usual modes of thought and speech of that time, are represented as suggested by an evil spirit,—in the repetition of, "*If thou be the Son of God,*" I read between the lines how deeply a new and overpowering sense of his Divine Sonship had been impressed upon his mind. And in the repeated mention of *stones* in the same account I read also how, in his self-communings, his thoughts were suggested by surrounding objects, and took shape therefrom. ("Command these *stones* to become bread," and "He will give his angels charge concerning thee, . . . lest at any time thou dash thy foot against a *stone*.")

The Gospels tell us only of those things which struck their authors as extraordinary. There are many little particulars which we should like now to know, of which they give us no information, as they were not thought to be worth mentioning. Thus, they have not told us how the experiences of Jesus at his baptism and in the Desert came to be known. That they were told by him to his disciples, I doubt not.

FIRST APPEARANCE IN PUBLIC.

The first public appearance of Christ as a teacher caused a sudden and great sensation, so new and commanding was the air of authority with which he bore himself. An insane man, who chanced to be present in the synagogue, supposed, according to the popular belief of the time, to be possessed by an evil spirit, was so excited by the whole appearance and discourse of Jesus that, unable to control himself, and breaking in upon the decorum of the place, he cried out in the character of the demon by whom he believed himself to be prompted, calling Jesus the Holy one of God. Jesus instantly turned upon the man his word and eye of command, and bade the evil spirit depart. Whereupon the man, under that influence, shrieked out and fell into convulsions, and shortly became calm and composed. The people present could have but one thought: Jesus was a powerful exorcist. From the synagogue Jesus, followed by an excited crowd, as I cannot but imagine, went to Peter's house, whither, doubtless, the rumor of the startling incident in the synagogue preceded him. Peter's mother-in-law was lying ill of a fever. At his appearance at her bedside, at the thrilling touch of his hand, so stimulated by the excitement of the moment were her vital forces, that she threw off her fever and was able to leave her bed and assist in the offices of hospitality. At sundown, when the Sabbath was past, a great crowd, "the whole city," one Gospel says, were gathered round the house.

Then we are told that the next morning Jesus *"rose a great while before day, and went out, and departed into a solitary place, and there prayed."* I read between the lines that he was so disturbed by what had happened the day before that he could not sleep, and was again "driven of the Spirit" into solitude, there to prepare himself by meditation and prayer for the unlooked-for turn which things had taken; and when his disciples went in search of him and found him and told him that every one was inquiring for him, in his refusal to return to Capernaum, where such a sensation existed, I read still further that he had a far higher purpose than the healing of bodily diseases.

Thus reading this passage, I find myself at a point of view from which all the difficulty about the miracles of Christ vanishes in the flood of new light shed upon those sudden and extraordinary effects which are so named. I see that they never were of his seeking, that he wrought them never for the sake of exhibiting his power, but only as he was moved by compassion, that they occurred wellnigh involuntarily on his part. He never went out of his way—he rather avoided occasions—for those marvels. He was at times impatient of them, seeing that they fed only a barren wonder. "Except you see signs and wonders," he once exclaimed, "you will not believe." They had not been contemplated by him when, previously to his appearance in public, he had meditated on his future. His thoughts and aspirations had, I repeat, far higher aims than the cure of bodily diseases, even the cure of souls.

And as these cures were mostly of a description susceptible of mental influence, I perceive with equal clearness that they admit of being referred to the unconscious power, the all-subduing charm, of the person of Jesus, signified in his whole bearing, in the expression of his countenance, in the thrilling tones of his voice, in the air of authority with which he spoke, and which was born of his profound conviction of truth, and was so striking that it is expressly mentioned as unlike anything that the people were accustomed to. "*He taught as one having authority, and not as the Scribes,*"—the only passage, I

FIRST APPEARANCE IN PUBLIC. 101

believe, approaching a description of him in all the Gospels.

Now, what we have all been taught is, that these remarkable effects were miracles in the sense of suspensions of the laws of nature, which Jesus was expressly empowered to work in order to prove that he was from God.

They certainly do attest that God was with him. But not because they were departures from the natural course of things, but for the very reverse. They show that, in conformity with the great law, the Divine way, in the spiritual world as in the physical, Jesus commanded Nature by obeying her. So true was he, in his whole bearing and being, to the highest and best in human nature, that, without design on his part, and to his own surprise, in the first instance, his simple appearance, the whole air of him, instantly inspired all, whose hearts were not turned into stone by spiritual pride and prejudice, with a boundless confidence. As the needle turns to the pole, so all that was true in the heart of man turned to him, even as he himself said: "Every true man hearkens to my voice." Even his judge, weak, unprincipled as that magistrate was, had that in him which was so touched by the appearance and behavior of Jesus that, calling all the people to witness, he cried, "I am guiltless of the blood of this innocent man!"

When this extraordinary, personal power, native to Christ as a man, is given full weight, it will be seen that there is no need of the supposition that he was preternaturally gifted. It abundantly suffices to account for the extraordinary impression that he made. This it was that called forth into all-conquering activity, in the sick and suffering especially, the most powerful principle in the constitution of man, Faith.

What is there more natural to man than Faith? He was created, born, to believe as surely as he was made to see with eyes. The Scripture saith, The just shall live by Faith. In truth, the unjust, we all, live by Faith. Upon what else does the world-embracing system of trade and commerce rest? It is Faith that is treading the mountains under foot, that summons the lightning to our service and it obeys. It is Faith that is preparing the highway of the Lord, making the paths straight for civilization and human brotherhood, and for all the great interests of mankind over all the land and through the deep places of the sea. To Faith we owe all discoveries, all progress. All things are possible to it, said Jesus. It commands all nature. To this mighty agent directly he ascribed the sudden and extraordinary effects which we call miracles. It restored health to the sick, sight to the blind, life to the dead.

Between the lines that report the emphatic and unqualified terms in which he described the power of Faith, in his declaration that, when it existed only as a grain of mustard-seed, it could uproot trees and toss mountains into the sea, I read farther, and it breaks upon me as a revelation, that, greatly as the people were moved by the wonders wrought, no one was so profoundly impressed by them as Jesus himself. So deep was the impression that they made on him—and herein the peerless strength of his character is seen—that, as unconscious of the power in him which produced them as he was of his breathing, so far from feeling one throb of self-elation, he no more thought of taking credit to himself for them, than of priding himself upon the action of his lungs. They simply brought him a new and all-inspiring experience, deepening his own faith mightily. The multitudes who witnessed them were filled with amazement. Insensible to their acclamations as though he heard them not, he had a vision of God in that wonder-working Faith, the presence of that Supreme Power, whose ways—the laws of nature we call them—are in the great deep of the human soul as they are everywhere throughout the Universe. It was in the conscious power of his own faith, quickened by what he witnessed, that he described faith in the strongest possible language. His own faith became one with his personal consciousness. Accordingly, he is never represented as appealing to any power external to himself. He uttered no adjurations. On no occasions did he speak in a more commanding tone of personal authority than when he healed the sick and summoned the dead back to life.

It is most interesting to note that his personal consciousness was not lost in the consciousness of the power of God within, but was rendered all the deeper by being identified therewith. He did not lose himself, he found himself, in God. When at last he cried, "*Not my will, but thine, be done!"* the apparent surrender of his own will was, in truth, the exaltation of it into perfect unity with the Divine Will.

Young and without any previous similar experiences, upon his first appearance in public, incidents, wholly unlooked for, occurred which called forth the wildest demonstrations of popular favor, and he instantly became the object of all men's wonder. The rumor of his acts and words ran far and wide, losing, we may be sure, nothing of the marvellous as it spread. Crowds flocked to him from all quarters. At one time, we are told, there was such "a coming and going" that he and those who attended him had not time " so much as to eat." Again the multitude was so great that they trampled upon one another. He had to keep a boat in waiting upon the shore of the Galilean lake, where he first appeared, that he might escape the press of the multitude. The whole country, wild with the sensation he was causing, heaved under his steps. He saw deranged minds, through the confidence reposed in him, restored to sanity, and withered limbs, and limbs swollen with leprosy, and sightless eyes, recover their soundness.

How could it be otherwise with him than I have said? Such an extraordinary state of things must have affected him deeply,—how deeply, we discover, I repeat, as we read between the lines that report the unqualified language in which he spoke of Faith.

His own faith in Faith being quickened, as I have described, there was created in him such a consciousness of power as only such a person, with such an extraordinary experience, could have. It was, I conceive, in the unparalleled energy of this faith that he called back the dead to life and awoke himself from the deep slumber.

It is comparatively easy to appreciate the greatness of mind which the last hours of his life illustrate, and which has transfigured the vile Cross into our most sacred symbol. But, in truth, the very beginning of his public life, when, in his youth and inexperience, he was confronted with such startling and unexpected incidents, manifests no less impressively the same Godlike character. He was alike unmoved by the horrors of a lonely and terrible death and by the blandishments of the most enthusiastic popular favor. The acclamations of multitudes made no impression on him. They passed by him as the idle wind. He was as deaf to those seducing voices at the first as he was to the imprecations of his priestly persecutors at the last. Both the one and the other serve only to illustrate his utter unconsciousness of the severe ordeal to which he was subjected. They illumined, but they could not embarrass, his perfect self-possession. As in the storm on the lake, he was alike unmoved by the wild war of the elements and by its sudden cessation, so that his terrified disciples rushed to the belief that there was an understanding between him and the winds and waves, and that they subsided at his rebuke, so always, from the first to the last, he shows a royal authority over the most trying circumstances, making them his obedient ministers, which if we fail to be struck with, it is because it was as naturally and uniformly sustained as if it were the merest matter of course, and nothing else were possible. We are insensible to it even as he himself was unconscious of it. Not until we recollect his temptations in the wilderness at the first and his agony in the garden at the last, are we made to see how entirely native to him his greatness was, and how the regal dignity of his mind was due to no phlegmatic insensibility, but to a character no less tender than strong.

On the Lake.

Where it is related that he was in a vessel on the lake, and that he was asleep, and that there were other boats out on the lake at the same time, we may read between the lines that, exhausted by the fatigue which drove him there to escape the crowds, he had instantly fallen asleep, and that, when he left the land, those other boats had pushed off, filled with people determined not to lose sight of him. These particulars are not mentioned, but are they not just as legible as the written characters?

Jesus and his Mother.

On a certain occasion, when Jesus was surrounded by a large crowd in a state of great excitement caused by a sudden cure that had just been wrought, and certain Pharisees present, stung to madness by hearing the people pronounce this base Galilean the son of David! the Messiah! charged him with being in league

JESUS AND HIS MOTHER. 109

with the very devil of devils, upon some one's calling out to him that his mother was there wanting to speak with him, he exclaimed, "*Who is my mother?*" an exclamation apparently so unfilial that M. Renan infers from it that he was wanting in natural affection,—He! he who, in the sharp agony of a terrible death, forgot himself in solicitude for her who bore him!

[That divinely human incident, by the way, at the Crucifixion M. Renan regards as a fabrication designed to intimate what a favorite of Jesus John was. This way of disposing of whatever in the history happens to strike us as unlikely is very easy, but, as I have said, the perfectly artless character of the Gospels peremptorily forbids recourse to any such suspicions. To return:]

Between the lines I read that his mother, alarmed at the stir which her son was causing, and fearing, from the malignant things said against him, that he would get himself into trouble, had come to persuade him to go home with her.

I read further that, shocked to the last degree at the depravity of ascribing to the devil an act of humanity, he was so carried away by his indignation in exposing the base charge, that it was not in human nature to regard the abrupt introduction, even of his dearest personal ties, otherwise than as an intolerable intrusion. I read in his exclamation, not that he loved his mother less than he should, but that he loved God and truth the most. We can love no mortal friend truly until we love God supremely.

In the third Gospel, where the same occurrence is related, there is nothing said of the mother of Jesus' wanting to see him, but it is written that a woman in the crowd cried aloud, "*Blessed is she who bore thee, and the breast that gave thee nourishment.*" Between the lines I read that it was hearing the mother of Jesus mentioned (as stated in the first Gospel) that suggested this woman's exclamation. And I read also in his reply to her, "*Blessed are they who hear the word of God and keep it,*" the same state of mind that a moment before led him to exclaim, "Who is my mother?" Any allusions to himself or to his private relations he could not then bear, so absorbed was he in exposing the blasphemy of attributing to an evil spirit the manifest work of God. Such allusions, diverting attention from the truths that he was then declaring, and that filled his whole mind, he felt to be ill-timed, utterly out of place.

When the scene ended by his pointing to his disciples, and saying, "Behold my mother and my brothers! Whosoever will do the will of my Father in heaven, the same is my mother, and *sister*, and brother,"—in this introduction of the sisterly relation is there not visible between the lines a reference to the woman who had just broken forth in blessing his mother? Do I fancy, or do I not read, that the woman, with the characteristic disposition of her sex, took his reply, "Blessed are they who hear the word of God and keep it," although expressed in general terms, directly to herself, as a personal rebuff, as if he had said, "Blessed art thou if thou hear the word of God and keep it," and that it was because he saw her and marked her discomfiture, or felt that she was wounded, that he introduced the sisterly allusion?

Jesus and the Rich Youth.

The narrative of the rich young man who came to Jesus, asking what he should do to inherit eternal life, abounds in exquisite touches, written between the lines, not by the hand of man, but by truth and nature.

To perceive the full significance of this passage, we must keep distinctly in mind the wide difference between Christ's idea of the Kingdom of Heaven, and the idea that his disciples had of it. To them it was a kingdom like all other kingdoms, only far excelling all others in wealth and power. To him it was the reign of Truth and Righteousness, which could be established, such were the corruptions of the world, such the savage passions that bore sway, only through the fire and blood of merciless persecutions. No one could engage in its service, who was not prepared to give up everything for its sake.

The appearance of the rich youth was so prepossessing that it is said, in the simple style of the Gospels, that "*Jesus loved him.*" His respectful address, " Good Master!" uttered in no hollow, conventional tone, but with that air of earnest sincerity that carries with it a certain authority, prompted Jesus to repel the winning flattery, to disclaim the title of " Good," and to

JESUS AND THE RICH YOUTH. 113

remind the youth that only to One did that title apply.

In answer to the question put to him, Jesus bade the young man keep the Commandments. "I have always kept them; what more am I to do?" was the further inquiry. "If thou wilt be perfect," said Jesus, "dispose of your riches, give them to the poor, and come with me."

It has been inferred from these words that Jesus required a vow of perpetual poverty as an essential condition of Christian discipleship. But he spoke for the hour. Now that he has not lived and died wholly in vain, the world is so far advanced, that wealth may be made a powerful means of aiding in the establishment of the Divine Kingdom. But at such a time as that in which Christ lived, no wiser counsel could be given than he gave to any one who proposed to devote himself to the advancement of Truth and Right; for the certain loss, not of property only, but of life would be incurred in that service. Upon no other condition at that time could the true Kingdom of God come.

The young man, accustomed to a life of luxury, was utterly unequal to so great a sacrifice. Give up all his riches! it was impossible. He had come running to Jesus with all the ardent confidence of youth, unconscious of ever having transgressed the law, ready, he flattered himself, to do whatever might be required of him for the sake of the life eternal. He turned crestfallen and went slowly away.

And then broke from the lips of Jesus the exclamation, "*How hardly shall they who have riches enter into the Kingdom of God!*" As if he had said, "Since this young man, blameless of any transgression, lovable as he is, cannot resign his riches for the Kingdom of Heaven's sake, no rich man can. A camel can pass through the eye of a needle sooner."

Jesus is greatly misunderstood when he is here taken to the letter. He spoke as he was moved. He was touched to the heart by the case of this interesting youth. It was deep feeling to which he thus gave expression; and deep feeling never limits itself to measured terms. It never stops to make exceptions, or to qualify its utterances. Not the absolute impossibility, but the extreme difficulty, of the entrance of the rich into the Kingdom of God, that is, into the self-sacrificing service of Truth at that hour, is the lesson we are to learn from these words of Christ's.

At this exclamation of his, his disciples were exceedingly astonished, as well they might be, seeing what their views were, and they cried, "Who then can be saved?" "To enter the Kingdom of Heaven" and "to be saved" were, in their minds, equivalent expressions. And salvation meant with them, first of all, salvation from poverty; it was to be made rich. They were, of course, amazed above measure at this declaration of their Master's. If the rich could not enter the glorious kingdom, could not be saved, such was their thought, how could there be any saved? Simple-minded men that they were! How transparently did they betray the childish dreams they were cherishing! Fixing his eyes upon them (with a look which they never forgot,—it is expressly recorded in two of the Gospels,—as if he were reading all that was in their hearts, and saw the whole extent of their delusion), well did he call them "Children," and, in answer to their looks and exclamations of wonder, assure them that it might be impossible to them that there should be any salvation without rich men, but that it was possible with God.

Wisely did he forbear, for their sakes, to go any further. Time and the progress of events, he well knew, would enlighten them, and bring them riches surpassing far their present worldly expectations. Any further explanation, at that moment, they could not bear. It would have been sure to shock them and peril their fidelity to the Truth.

Reading on between the lines, we have a still fuller revelation of their hopes, when Peter, ever forward to take the lead and speak for the others, thinking it high time to come to an understanding, immediately inquired, "What are we going to have, we who have left all and followed thee?" "*Verily, I say unto you,*" answered their Master, "*there is no man who has left house, or parents, or brothers, or sisters, or wife, or children, for the Kingdom of God's sake, who will not receive manifold more in this present time, and in the world to come life everlasting.*" An eternal truth. An emphatic announcement of the law of compensation. Whatever a man sacrifices for God and the Right, Truth will do manifold more for him than he can do for the Truth. That will reward him in full measure, pressed down and running over.

The disciples of Jesus, however, could not then have caught so much as an inkling of his meaning. Of "the peace and joy in believing" which they afterwards came to know, they had as yet no experience. They were confidently expecting to be rewarded for their devotion to their Master with riches and honors. They had no thought of the possibility of any different compensation. Accordingly, in the first Gospel we find Jesus reported as saying, not what he said, but what, in their simplicity, they honestly believed that he meant, namely, that they should "*sit on twelve thrones, judging the twelve tribes of Israel.*" With their expectations, they could put no other construction upon "the manifold more" which he promised, a construction which I cannot for a moment imagine that he dreamed of authorising. It contradicts the whole tenor of his teaching, the whole spirit of his life. And, besides, it is directly at variance with the warning that he immediately gave them, that though they were the first they might be the last.

Since Peter and his fellow-disciples, as may be

read between the lines, were flattering themselves with the expectation that as they were the first to follow Christ, they would have an advantage over those who came after them, he went on to say that many, who were first, would be last, and the last would be first. And in illustration of this saying he told the story of the owner of a vineyard, who went out at different hours of the day to hire laborers, and at the end of the day paid those whom he had engaged at the eleventh hour equally with the first; a parable that has been held to teach the efficacy of a death-bed repentance. It has no such reference. The eleventh hour laborers had not refused to work before. They had had no opportunity. No man had hired them. What the story was intended to teach is that those who should, in the Providence of Heaven, come late into the service of the Divine Kingdom, would share in the rewards of that service equally with those who came earlier. Had the disciples perceived the drift of the parable, they would not have expected a reward for being the first.

Let us pause here to observe with what fidelity to nature the spiritual growth of the personal disciples of Christ went on. Much of what he said, they scarcely, if at all, understood. It was utterly irreconcilable with all their fondly cherished views. It found no place in minds full of very different things. Nevertheless, his personal influence, acting upon them every instant, unconsciously on his part and on theirs, through every glance of his eye and every tone of his voice, was steadily creating in them a growing trust, a respect that deepened into awe, and they learned to confide in him more than in themselves. In contradiction of a common proverb, the more familiar and intimate their intercourse with him, the profounder grew their reverence. But the more they trusted in him, the more passionately did they cherish their Messianic visions. Thus the tares and the wheat grew together in their minds, and for a while, instead of either's choking the other, they promoted each the other's growth. As their worldly hopes grew, so grew the faith of his disciples in Christ. It became necessary for their sakes, as he is recorded to have told them, that he should leave them, that the right spirit might gain the ascendency. Although they never formally renounced their Jewish expectations, and though to the last they looked for their Master to come again and reign in great glory, yet the vision retreated into the background, and the vile Cross became more glorious in their eyes than any throne. The wheat outgrew the tares.

Jesus at Bethany.

What a truth to nature, what a depth of pathos, do we miss when we read only what is written, and discern not what is legible between the lines in the account of what passed in the house of Simon at Bethany, where Mary, in token of her reverence, poured the precious ointment on the head of Jesus!

There may seem at first sight an inconsistency between his ready acceptance of that costly act of personal homage and his disclaiming expressions of personal respect as he did, once, when, as we have seen, he was accosted by the title of "Good Master," and again when a woman broke forth in a benediction on his mother. But all appearance of inconsistency vanishes when we note the peculiar circumstances of the occasion in Simon's house.

The incident at Bethany occurred only a short time before the death of Jesus, when the black shadow of his awful fate was upon him. Aware that his powerful enemies were busy conspiring against him and that he might be arrested at any moment and dragged away to death, was it not in exquisite accord with human nature that he should be struck by the connection of this act of Mary with his near death? The perfume of the ointment, associated by the custom of his people with the offices for the dead, filled his sense with the odor of death and of the grave. Had a thought of the construction which he put upon this act of hers crossed the mind of Mary, how would she have shrunk from thus hastening to discharge so painful an office! She thought only of doing him honor. It was because she did not dream of what she was doing that he was so struck with the connection of her act with his near death, that he declared it would be told all the world over. She was performing a more sacred office than she knew. She was embalming him. "Disturb her not!" he exclaimed.

As he had lived, so was he about to die for

the poor, for the poor of all ages and all climes. But, at that moment, the claims of the poor were to be set aside. A purpose of affection, sacred in itself, and doubly sacred in that it was undesignedly a solemn funeral office, was not to be frustrated. The poor could always be ministered to; but the fragrance, that then filled one humble dwelling, was to fill all the world, and the pathos of that act of Mary, that never could be repeated, was to touch the hearts of generations of men.

At the Last Supper.

In the thirteenth chapter of the fourth Gospel it is written that Jesus "*rose from supper, and laid aside his garments, and took a towel, and girded himself. After that he poured water into a basin,*" etc. Here is a detail of apparently insignificant particulars, curiously minute. We read between the lines that the wonder of what followed began with his rising from the table. All eyes were instantly turned to him. "What is he going to do?" was written on every face. Every movement that he made, increasing the wonder and curiosity with which it was watched, stamped itself on the minds of all present as an inseparable part of the menial office which he ended with discharging, and at which all but one were struck dumb.

Upon the same memorable evening, how manifest, as we read on between the lines, is the reluctance with which he discloses his knowledge of the meditated treachery of one of their number! That their faith in him might not be shaken, that they might know that he was not going to be taken by surprise, that he was prepared for what was to befall, he deemed it necessary that he should tell them that there was a traitor among them. Twice he alluded to it, more pointedly the second time than the first. At last, in agitation and distress of mind, he said outright that one of them was about to prove false to him. He mentioned no name. Only in a whisper to John, who leaned on his bosom, did he point out the traitor, but not then by name, but by a sign, lest the others, who were watching him, might catch the name from the motion of his lips.

Again. What a world of faith and reverence is revealed in the cry, "*Lord, is it I?*" that broke forth all around the table, when he made this communication! Innocent of any thought of treachery as all but one of them were conscious of being, their instant conviction was that their Master knew them better than they knew themselves, and that they might be guilty of the black crime sooner than he could bring against them a groundless accusation.

The Raising of Lazarus.

In the narrative of the Raising of Lazarus, there is nothing said of the immediate effect of the wonder upon the spectators. But when it is stated that at the appearance of the man alive at the entrance of the sepulchre, Jesus said, "Loosen him, that he may walk," we read between the lines that all present were standing, transfixed with amazement, motionless as statues, staring with eyes starting from their sockets at the blindfolded apparition staggering in the voluminous folds of the shroud, till Jesus broke the spell by bidding them go to the assistance of his risen friend.

In the same wonderful narrative, wonderful not only for the extraordinary event which it relates, but for the inimitable marks of truth and of nature with which it is inlaid, when it is said that Jesus called with a loud voice to the dead man to come forth, I read as plainly as if it were written in visible characters, that Jesus called thus aloud in perfect faith, that is, he called with a loud voice, believing, knowing, that the dead would hear him.

As in death all signs of life cognizable to our limited vision, which perceives only the surfaces of things, disappear, we rashly assume that death is absolute extinction. But we do not know either what death is or life, or to what extent the one is affected by the other. Neither do we know what hidden sympathies there may be between the living and the dead, especially when the living and the dead are bound together by the ties of such a friendship as united Jesus and Lazarus.

Were we only penetrated with a due sense of our very limited knowledge, we might be ready to confess that death is an unsolved secret, and be in no haste to pronounce incredible the instances of the dead recalled to life recorded in the Gospels. We might be induced to ponder them thoughtfully. We could hardly fail to be impressed by the simple, direct manner of Jesus in working these wonders, in consummate harmony as it is with the perfect dignity of his character, and with the inimitable simplicity of nature as well.

I cannot but think that, if the story of the Raising of Lazarus were a fiction, the creation of the love of the wonderful, he who recalled the dead to life would hardly have been represented as requiring the aid of human hands to remove the stone from the sepulchre, nor would the dead man have been described as instantly needing assistance upon his appearance alive.

Duly appreciating the internal evidences of the truth of these narratives of the dead restored to life by Christ, we might obtain some insight into what death is, and accept these facts as decisive proof that there is a life hidden in the mortal body, which that mysterious change cannot harm, and which, under the conditions that existed in the cases recorded in the Gospels, can, for a period more or less limited, regain its command over the body and revive it.

The notices of the sisters of Lazarus, Martha

and Mary, in the narrative of their brother's restoration, are wonderfully in harmony with what is related of them elsewhere in the Gospels. They are nowhere described. It is nowhere said what manner of persons they were. Only one or two slight incidents, in which they are the actors, are related. And yet, reading between the lines, we get from those incidents ideas of the respective characters of these two women as distinct as if we were personally acquainted with them.

And here I must repeat what I have said about them more than once before. The interest of the subject is my apology.

Martha was the first to go and meet Jesus when she heard he was coming, because, " cumbered with much serving," she was in that part of the house where the intelligence of his approach would be first received. Mary was in a retired room indulging her grief, as her characteristic sensibility prompted, and the custom of the time allowed. Martha could not have forgotten her sister, but she neither went nor sent to let Mary know that Jesus was at hand. She started off by herself to meet him. And it is so in character with the jealousy of her sister shown on the only other occasion in which she appears in the history, that we may naturally surmise that she went off by herself without a word to her sister, whose reverence for Jesus she well knew, that she might have him all to herself without Mary by. When Jesus was with them and Mary was present, conversing with him as Martha could not, the practical, matter-of-fact character of Martha authorises the suspicion that she had an uncomfortable feeling of inferiority, especially if she were the elder. Whether older than Mary or not, she was probably accustomed, by virtue of her practical temperament, and Mary's indifference to household cares, to take the lead in domestic concerns, and, therefore, it was not agreeable to her, especially when guests were in the house, to appear to occupy a subordinate position. She had not liked to see Mary sitting still at the feet of Jesus while she had her hands full of work, preparing, as he told her, more than enough, for the table. I suppose if Mary had been bidden by Jesus to help Martha, Martha would only have found her in the way.

When Martha met Jesus, how plainly is it writ between the lines that she was wholly unable to sustain any conversation with him! Everything he said staggered her. She could not take in what he said. When he told her her brother would rise again, she shrank from the idea, and sought relief from so great a thought in her traditional faith in the final resurrection. And when he went on to say (in those profoundly significant words) that he was the resurrection and the life, and, virtually, that her brother, though dead, yet having had faith in him, still lived, and that she herself, living and believing in him, would never die, and then demanded of her whether she believed this, again, confounded by the new, great thoughts that he presented, she took refuge in a general confession of faith in him as the Messiah,—and retreated. Do we not read, though it is not written in so many words, that he startled and overpowered her? He was too much for her. She could not talk with him. She left his presence, and went and told Mary that Jesus had come, and that she was wanted. Mary would understand him, she could not. So she was forced to feel; and the virtual confession of her incompetency which she had to make in having to call Mary, could not, chagrined as she was, be uttered aloud. And therefore it was that she spoke to Mary "*secretly*," in a whisper.

Again we read Martha's nature in the objection she interposed to the removal of the stone from the tomb,—as if Jesus did not know what he was doing. Mary's silence speaks, and tells us more significantly than any words what manner of person she was.

Never, in any work of fiction, with strokes so few and delicate, has personal character been so exquisitely and yet incidentally portrayed. In the same way the distinctive features of Peter and Pilate are rendered as recognizable as those of familiar personal acquaintances.

The friendship subsisting between Jesus and the family of Lazarus is a fact of no slight interest, bearing witness as it does to the large and liberal spirit of Jesus. Devoted heart and soul to his great work, naturally eager as he must have been to obtain fellow-workers, he was no zealot, insisting upon adhesion to himself as the indispensable condition of his personal friendship. He warned all who would join him to count the cost. He had friends, it appears, in private life who took no public part with him. He was not blind to the fact that it was not given to every one to share in his labors and sacrifices.

The Silence of Jesus.

In the silence which Jesus preserved when arraigned before the Roman governor, and the Priests were clamoring for his crucifixion, when not a word of fear, not an ejaculation for mercy, not a syllable of self-exculpation was breathed from his lips,—in his demeanor in those awful circumstances I read a great deal more than a lamb-like submission to slaughter. I behold a conscious rectitude, a pride of virtue, a royal greatness of mind, with which the annals of mankind may be challenged to produce a parallel.

Alone, with not a soul in all the world that understood him, defamed, ridiculed, denounced as the enemy of God and of man, with savage bigotry and hate raging against him, he stood there, wrapt around in the robes of angelic innocence and truth. He could not descend to bandy words with those, whom if words could have moved from their fell purpose, those words had already been uttered. Whatever he could have said then would only exasperate their malice. His blood was the only answer that remained to be given to their calumnies, and that answer centuries were to accept as his triumphant vindication. For that supreme moment, silent communion with himself and with the Infinite Father was alone fitted.

Oh, it is not for any words that he spoke, surpassingly wise as these are, it is for his bearing, more divinely glorious than any aureole could symbolize, then, and always, that we are moved to exclaim, in revering admiration, "Truly, this is the Son of God!"

Baptism and the Lord's Supper.

Reading always, not only what is written, but what is plainly legible between the lines, we gather from the Gospels that Christ instituted no peculiar forms of doctrine or of observance, neither a creed nor a ritual.

We have, it is true, our so-called Christian Institutions, accepted as resting upon his explicit authority by all denominations, except the Friends: Baptism and the Lord's Supper.

Baptism was a rite familiar to the countrymen of Jesus before he appeared. He observed it himself, but he never baptised any one (John iv, 2). Had he designed it to be what it is now accounted, a necessary, initiatory ceremony, it is incredible that there should be no mention of any such purpose either in the third or the fourth Gospel, and that in the first and second Gospels he is said only once in each to have enjoined its observance, and that briefly and at the very last. His disciples baptised, but it does not appear that it was in obedience to any injunction of his. In the particular instructions (Matth. x,) which he gave them when he sent them forth to herald the glad tidings, there is no word about Baptism.

These things being considered, it is much more probable that the command to baptise, recorded only once in the final verses of Matthew and Mark, crept into the text from the margin of some early copy of those Gospels, than that it should have been really given by Christ.

It should be remembered that before the manufacture of copies of the Gospel narratives passed into the hands of professional and paid transcribers, the first copies that were made were made in all probability by individuals for themselves or for their friends (as Luke wrote his Gospel for his friend Theophilus), not mechanically, but with the liveliest interest in their contents, prompting them occasionally to put a word or two, here and there, in the margin, by way of comment or explanation; and then, when other copies were made from theirs, these marginal notes would be apt to be transferred into the text, with no ill design, but under the impression that they belonged there and had been omitted through carelessness. This is one of the ways in which Biblical critics account for certain probable corruptions of the text. Indeed, the last twelve verses of the second Gospel, which include the mention of Baptism, are of doubtful genuineness, and they are so indicated in the Revised Version of the New Testament.

If, however, Christ enjoined Baptism, it may be questioned whether, in the passages where alone it is mentioned, he is to be taken to the letter, or figuratively, that is, as he used the word when he said he had a baptism to suffer, and again, when he asked James and John if they were prepared, with him, for the same baptism. It was in the same figurative sense that his Precursor, the Baptist, used the word when he said to the people that he baptised them with water, but that there was one coming mightier than he, who would baptise them with the holy spirit and with fire. Water, that cleanses only outwardly, was the symbol of the Baptist's influence. But the power of him who was about to appear would be signified by more searching elements, spirit and fire. [It is impossible to convey in any one English word the full meaning of the Greek word πνεῦμα, here translated *spirit*. It is expressive of the power as well as of the subtilty of Air. In one and the same verse (John iii, 8) it is translated both wind and spirit: "The *wind* bloweth where it listeth . . . so is every one that is born of the *spirit*."] The Baptist, who held Jesus in the deepest reverence, as appears from his not thinking himself worthy to baptise him, spoke, I doubt not, from personal experience when he said that Jesus would baptise with the spirit and with fire. To Jesus, I believe, he referred when he spoke of him who was coming. He had felt the power of Jesus. In previous communings with his great kinsman he had experience of a spiritual and kindling baptism. Such and no outward rite was the Baptism that Jesus sent forth his Apostles to administer. Certain it is that Paul did not consider himself required to baptise with water, although commissioned directly by Christ himself. He thanked God that he had baptised only two or three persons in Corinth (1 Cor. i, 17).

Of the Lord's Supper so called, no mention is made in the fourth Gospel; and this Gospel is ascribed to the beloved disciple. In the first and second Gospels, there is not a syllable intimating a thought on Christ's part of instituting a commemorative rite. In Luke only we have the words, "*Do this in remembrance of me.*" Were the observance of the essential importance ascribed to it, it is not credible that so slight a ground should exist for it. Considering the silence of the other Gospels on this point, and how needless any express injunction to a special remembrance of him was subsequently proved to be, since a commemorative observance sprang up by the pure force of nature, of itself, as it were, and took form from the striking incident of his last supper with his disciples, we may well conclude that, arising so naturally, it was taken for granted that the observance must have been expressly enjoined by Christ; and thus the words in Luke, written first, probably, in the margin of some copy, passed into the text of subsequent MSS.

After the disappearance of their Master, whenever the disciples met to eat and drink together, they could not fail to recall those remarkable words of his about the bread and wine on the occasion of their last meal with him. Thus, not by convention nor by formal institution, but like all observances that have life in them, "out from the heart of Nature" sprang our Memorial Service.

So, in the same way, the first day of the week grew to be commemorative of the greatest event in the history of Christ, his Resurrection, and became a formal service, instituted by Nature, and entitled the Master's or Lord's day.

Jesus himself, I conceive, had as little thought of instituting the Lord's Supper as he had of making the first day of the week a day to be set apart and formally observed. The occasion of his last supper with his humble friends was an occasion of the deepest emotion to him. He knew that it was the last. His awful fate was on the eve of its consummation. Images of the near horror rose with appalling effect before his mind. So vividly did the broken bread and the flowing red wine call up before him his lacerated body and streaming blood, that the signs vanished from his sight before the things signified, and, shocked to the last degree, he exclaimed, "It is my body!" "It is my blood!" He could not drink of the wine, nor eat of the bread. It would be drinking his own blood, eating his own flesh. His was no state of mind for the institution of a formal ceremony.

I am misunderstood if it is inferred from what I say that I would abolish our Christian Commemorative Service. On the contrary, I would have it seen that it rests, not on the ground of formal institution, but upon the strongest possible ground of Nature.

As to the manner in which, and the frequency with which, it should be kept, these are open

JESUS INSTITUTED NO FORMS. 139

questions to be decided by the spirit of the time. It appears that at the first, the disciples made every occasion when they met to eat and drink together, commemorative of their last supper with him.

As he instituted no set forms, it is equally important to observe, neither did he forbid any. He neither commanded nor forbade his disciples to baptise. If at any time the observance of a baptismal form tends to deepen the sense of personal duty, then is Baptism a Christian observance.

Religious institutions, creeds, and ceremonials, mankind always have had, and always will have, so long as a sense of religion is an essential element of human nature. If there are any wearing the human shape who acknowledge no Power above them, and are conscious of no sentiment of religious faith or fear, they are, as Hume long ago said, on a level with the brutes. The philosophers of our day, who are sounding the deeps of human knowledge and who seem to imagine that they have struck bottom, no less than the most devout of worshippers, would fain have, as it now appears, their ceremonials and commemorative services, rivalling the Roman Catholic Church in the multitude of their Saints' days.

Since these things are so, since such is the constitution of man, and there will forever be forms of religion, it may be said that Christ left all such things to take care of themselves. He neither created nor forbade any peculiar religious institutions. It was no purpose of his to do away with such as existed.

A Religion, however, sprang from him, no creation of the wisdom of man, but rooted deep in nature, born of God. Its conception was immaculate. It is clothed with the highest possible authority. It is not a form, but a life, a spirit, a spirit of Love, of Liberty, of Power. Countless are the errors that have usurped its name and clogged its progress. But it lives, pure and undefiled, in Christ, its most luminous illustration. He came, as he said, not to destroy, but to fulfil, not to build a new religion upon the destruction of the old, but to breathe into the existing religion of his country and through that into all the world the spirit of his own broad humanity.

He threw the whole power of his great life and death into the supreme love of the Highest and Best and the fraternal love of man. Wherever these are the all-commanding affections, be the outward forms of Religion what they may, Christ and Christianity do not condemn those forms. Baptism, the Lord's Supper, and whatever observances minister to enlarge the heart towards God and man, are all Christian institutions.

Forms of theology and worship that educate the highest and best in our nature will be as diverse as the minds of men. When all are striving to give expression to one and the same religious sense, and by expressing to strengthen it, such are the constitutional differences among men, they must needs adopt different modes of thought and worship. Were it otherwise, it would not be in harmony with the infinite variety so dear to the Creator.

There is then the peace and joy of a divine charity in the faith in which we may rest, that the various forms of religion do all at least keep the religious sentiment alive. But there is a deeper peace still, a greater joy in the faith that there is a power in the world, the spirit, of which Christ is our divinest symbol, ever present as the oxygen of the atmosphere, which is penetrating and moulding them all in various degrees, and that every religion outside of Christendom as well as within its pale has its saints. The growing intercourse of Christian and non-Christian peoples, which there is now so much to facilitate, the treaties made between them in the interests of civilisation, abolishing slavery, for example, bear witness to the spirit of Christ, breathing a deeper life into the world.

It is only when creeds and rituals are exalted above the two great Commandments, or put on a level with them, that Christ condemns them. Then we hear his voice reiterating the ancient immortal word, "I will have humanity and not sacrifice."

I HAVE given in the preceding pages some instances of the way in which the Gospel narratives are to be read. I claim no novelty for the method I have observed. They are read in the same way by all who endeavor to read them understandingly and not by rote.

It has been objected that I interpret them arbitrarily, according to my liking, without reference to any sound principles of criticism. I can only repeat that I am not aware of having resorted to any far-fetched or fanciful suggestions. By the same way that I have followed in exhibiting the truth contained in these Writings, certain passages are found to be legendary, or exaggerations of ordinary events, such as, for instance, the story of the Nativity, the Transfiguration, and the Storm on the Lake.

If there is anything peculiar in the expositions which I have given, it is that I bring more fully into view than is commonly done, that Christ was a human being, a man, susceptible of human emotions, actuated by human feelings. This simple fact, when once it is taken fully into account, will make the history as luminous in its self-evidence as the sun, which needs no argument of its reality.

I do not profess to be able to set forth all the internal evidence, whether of fact or of fable, in the Gospels. That will require a keener eye than mine. But so far as I have come to know their real character, I have found them most original and wonderful in this, that they are as pure pieces of nature as any things in nature, as natural as the trees and the flowers. They are not a manufacture, but a growth. There breathes through them the same Divine Life that animates the whole creation.

Nature abounds in marvels. Among them, I hold the New Testament histories to be not the least, marvels of simplicity. It is a great mistake to think it would have been better had the accounts of Christ been written by educated persons. The more simple-natured, the more unsophisticated their authors, the easier is it to divine what it was that they actually saw and felt. No arts of literary composition color or refract the pure light of human nature shining through these simple narratives.

Were they mere human fabrications, they never would admit of being harmonised with the truth of nature. That man can mix artificial flowers with natural ones,—interpolate the crude creations of his ignorant love of the marvellous into the Divine Order of the world, so that no eye shall be able to see the difference between the two, is, to my mind, utterly beyond belief.

Conclusion.

We must set no limits to the Infinite Grace of God. The prophecy of the Apostle will be fulfilled. As God lives, the time must come when the spirit of Christ shall have subdued all that is hostile to it, and God will be all in all. No eye hath seen, no ear heard, no heart conceived, what is prepared in the counsels of the Infinite Father for his human family, what fuller revelations will be made, what loftier angels will appear with the messages of his Love, and do greater works than yet have been done or imagined. Science, as well as Scripture, inspires the faith that ever higher forms of life and good are to be evolved.

The time is not yet. Hardly does its coming shine even from afar. Only to the eye of faith is it visible. For the redemption of a world still lying in ignorance and sin, we look to Him who lived and died and rose again from the dead for the re-creation of mankind. Already has his influence been realised in countless redeeming agencies. But not only thus indirectly, but by his own personal power, shall he yet move the world. That power is far from being spent. He shall come again, not visibly to mortal eyes, not in the clouds of heaven, but, emerging from the blinding mists of theological and legendary theories, he will come, in the all-subduing power of his personal character, to create a new faith in God and in man.

In the mean while, everywhere now sectarian distinctions are magnified, and creeds and rituals usurp supremacy, engendering mutual contempt and hatred, and obstructing the genial circulation of the spirit of Christ. The Church, the most venerable for its age, the most imposing for the grandeur of its organization, for the multitudes of its members, and for the illustrious and saintly characters that appear within its pale, takes the lead in exalting forms and traditions above humanity and the love of God, sanctifying the sprinkling of a few drops of water, for example, with an efficacy so sacred that only by the antenatal administration of the rite of Baptism are unborn babes to be saved from everlasting perdition.

In this state of things can we consent to suffer the personality of Christ, at the first so powerful, to fade away into a fable? For ages his human person has been all but lost, through the distorting medium of dogmas so bewildering to the understanding, so powerless to reach the heart, that, save through the Crucifix and the Madonna with the infant Jesus, hardly a glimpse of his divine humanity could be caught; and the heart has turned to the Virgin Mother to slake its thirst for an object of veneration and trust, that appeals to those sentiments at once the most universal and the most powerful principles of human nature. Now that, by the Grace of God, we have been brought to reject as alike irrational and unscriptural the metaphysical representations of Christ which have so long and so widely prevailed, now, in fine, that we see what he was not, shall we be content to rest in this negative conclusion and never care to inquire what he positively was? Shall we be willing to remain in doubt whether his existence be not lost in a cloud of fable?

If there were no other inducement, simple curiosity, one would think, should prevent us from allowing to pass into neglect and oblivion the memory of one whose appearance in the world has determined the whole subsequent course of the world's history, and from the date of whose birth the most advanced nations count the years, as if all that preceded that event passed for nothing. Surely it could have been no fabulous personage—or all that is, is a delusion—whose presence in the world has had these consequences, no ordinary man, the representation of whom as no less a person than Almighty God himself has been and still is received as credible.

But the endeavor to ascertain who and what Christ was has a far higher motive than the gratification of mere curiosity. In the name of all that is just, generous, honorable, for God's sake and for man's, let us not forget the sacred debt that we owe to Christ himself. Before we consent that the divine Idea of him shall fade away from the minds of men, now that we are sufficiently enlightened to perceive how mournfully his person has for long ages been misunderstood, we are bound to see to it that justice be done to him.

When this is done, when he shall be known as he truly was, in the beauty of his Life, as human as it is Godlike, blessed will be the result. The world shall be like him when it sees him as he is. Revered as the realisation of the highest idea of human nature, the veneration, the faith in God and man, the love, the hope, that he will inspire, will prove to be, far more effectually than they ever yet have been since the Apostolic age, most powerful ministers of Heaven in cleansing and renovating mankind.

As these sentiments are awakened, as men are brought to see in him the Divinity of the nature which they share with him and to cherish self-respect and the sacred feeling of human respect, the more plainly will it appear that, however numerous and strongly marked are our differences of language, of customs and manners, and of religion, men everywhere, after all, are more alike than different, that their differences strike us as great because they are on the surface,—in fine, that as face answers to face in a mirror, so does the inmost heart of man to man.

And the means of human intercourse, now in ceaseless and increasing activity, and powerful beyond the dreams of the boldest imagination less than a century ago, are bringing men face to face, every man to see himself in his brother, and to labor together for the common welfare of mankind.

As mutual knowledge and respect increase, differences, now unduly magnified, and which only generate ill blood,—all, in short, that is not rooted in truth and nature, will wither away. It will not be plucked up by violence, by hands bathed in blood, as some madly dream, neither will it be out-argued. It will be outgrown. As in the case of the personal disciples of Christ, the wheat, Heaven-sown and fostered by the fruitful influences of Providence and of Nature, will choke the tares.

Of this, the Divine method in the regeneration alike of the individual and of the world at large, what an impressive instance have we had in the history, in this country, of the sacred Cause of Justice and Humanity, in which the well-being, not of one race or class, but of all mankind, was involved, as, for thirty years, it was steadily winning its way till the crisis came! As individuals of different religious names became interested in it, how soon were religious differences ignored, and with what mutual confidence did believers and unbelievers, so called, work together as brothers! Thus it has always been when any great vital issues were in question, when any deep feeling has stirred the minds of men. At the height of the great plague in the seventeenth century in London, the flood of one common fear submerged all sectarian distinctions, and the people rushed to implore the mercy of Heaven into the churches, regardless of the religious names the churches bore. So here, all thoughts of religious differences were swept away when the Spirit of Freedom and Humanity began to overflow the land.

As it has been, so will it be. All hearts are fashioned alike, and, notwithstanding all differences of forms of faith and worship, all shall become one in Christ. What is the chaff to the wheat? saith the Lord.

www.ingramcontent.com/pod-product-compliance
Lightning Source LLC
Chambersburg PA
CBHW030338170426
43202CB00010B/1161